THE MAN FROM HIGHBELOW

THE AUTOBIOGRAPHY OF ROBERT J. WOLFF

**Edited by
Dina Wolff, M.A.**

authentic.

FOREWORD

By Guy Wolff

FINDING HIGHBELOW

In the early seventies, as my father's physical strength was beginning to wane, he took to looking back over his life's work and came across the box holding *The Man From Highbelow*. His excitement over this discovery is what I remember most of that moment, and was the impetus for his writing about his life before finding his path as a painter.

I would say my father's creative life was motivated by his search for anything resonating truth and integrity. His instant fascination with *Highbelow*, a manuscript he did not remember writing, and its intent to search for a place of truth, shows how that search remained a constant in his life.

Over and over again my father made trouble for himself in the world of Gallery and Museum. To look back on his actions, he seemed determined to close the very doors that would put him in good stead, but how he came to the world was more important to him than where he got to. This moral stance itself, among his contemporaries, gave him even more trouble. In looking closer at *The Man From Highbelow*, I get a better picture of what he was up to, and in his actions why he came at the world the way he did.

My father's work kept him alive through decades of illness. He was at peace only in his beloved studio. He had the only true sense of being "home" when he was "with his work." Losing Highbelow, his spiritual home, was the catalyst of a life's work, and finding Highbelow, in that work, was its own reward.

◻◻◻

Wolff would be so happy and proud to see this work brought forward by the hard labor of his granddaughter, Dina. The connection between them has always been a joy for our whole family, and is alive and well.

To all who are inspired by R.J.W.'s path, I know he would say, "It's your turn, and good hunting."

Guy Wolff
Bantam, CT

ACKNOWLEDGMENTS

I would like to acknowledge my father, Dr. Stephen K. Blumberg, for his selfless, tireless contribution to this project. He is a man of great generosity, patience, humility, and enthusiasm. I would like also to thank my mother, Wendy Wolff Blumberg. Those who have been fortunate enough to find themselves turning the pages of this book must know that without their strong support of my efforts over the past decade, *The Man From Highbelow,* as you now see and touch it, would never have come to fruition.

回回回

This book is dedicated to fathers and grandfathers everywhere.

INTRODUCTION

By Dina Wolff

MY SEARCH FOR *THE MAN FROM HIGHBELOW*

If you are holding this book in your hands, you probably already have some idea who Robert J. Wolff is. What you likely don't know is how what you hold came into being. It's an interesting story, if I do say so myself, and it began way back in 1986 when I, his granddaughter, felt an urge to know who this blood relative artist was. In this introduction, I will explain how this urge surfaced and how that longing led me to find the manuscript you are about to read.

🔲🔲🔲

AT ABOUT AGE 24 OR 25 my curiosity about my Grandfather Wolff was born. I remember quite clearly the sunny afternoon, up in my childhood bedroom where I was living at the time, when this sudden desire arose to ask my mother about her father, my Grandpa Wolff, the man on whose birthday I was born, the man who left this planet when I was just 12 years-old. I ran down the stairs, found Mom, and asked if she had anything from or about Grandpa that might help me know him better. A short while later, she presented me with a stack of letters that my grandfather had written to me and my brothers, my mom and dad, and one or two to my Grandma Alice, his first wife, and her mother, my "Nana." But rather than appeasing my need to know Grandpa, those letters served as kindling that lit a raging fire inside my soul that, though greatly diminished now, nearly 15 years later, still burns.

Soon after the letters' discovery, I visited Mom's cousin Peter Eising in Seattle, for Cousin Peter was like a brother to Mom, an only child, and had spent time with Grandpa both as a child and an adult. Peter had told me that Grandpa had written this sort of autobiography called *The Man From Highbelow*, and he thought that maybe it was up in the attic. When I visited, we might be able to find it. But no such luck; Grandpa's life story was not in Seattle.

I returned to California without feeling discouraged, for there was much to learn. Someday I would get my hands on that manuscript, but in the meantime, I would put my energy into studying the art and history in which Grandpa had flourished. And I would find people who knew him and interview them. Maybe someday I would write Grandpa's biography, so any work in that direction would not be wasted.

In 1989, I went to New York where I indeed got to interview three very different people who had known Grandpa. Armed with a tiny recorder, I found my way around that metropolis, viewing the eight paintings that the Guggenheim owns and has stored in various warehouses, and listening to the three interviewees talk about Grandpa. I spoke with one of Grandpa's colleagues from Brooklyn College (Professor Milton Brown), a protege from that same institute, and a supposed old family friend. The five-day trip was a sure success. On my way back to California, I stopped in Chicago to get my Grandma Alice's take on Wolff, which proved to be another very different, but important interview. She was generous with me and provided a unique angle to the story of my grandfather's life.

That summer, I completed a U.C.L.A. extension course in Modern Art History and landed an editorial job at a travel magazine in San Francisco. For the next four years, aside from taking another Art History class during a year of film school (1991-1992) in anticipation of one day making a documentary film on my grandfather, my exploration took a sabbatical. It wasn't until Summer 1993 that I once again headed east, this time to Connecticut where Wolff's son, my Uncle Guy Wolff, lived, along with all of Grandpa's paintings and drawers of archival material, including, Uncle Guy had assured me, that manuscript, *The Man From Highbelow*.

◫ ◫ ◫

GUY PICKED ME UP at the bus depot, and drove me to his home in Bantam about a half hour away, where for the next three weeks I pretty much lived in the "barn," the structure he had built to house Grandpa's paintings. It was in this single room wood A-frame with the sheepskin rugs that I discovered and copied dozens of files Grandpa had meticulously organized before his death in 1977. According to Guy, Grandpa had been so diligent with his files because he expected that someday someone would write his biography. There even existed a file marked "Professional Biographical Data."

Stepping into the barn was like crossing into a magical world that, until age thirty-one, had been off limits. Each morning was like Christmas as I anticipated the moment when I would enter paradise, like a kid running downstairs to unwrap her presents. The first day was obviously the most shocking, for that was the day of discovery: files and files of letters, poetry, notes, lectures, fiction, essays, and articles. And there amongst them all, in a dusty box, I found it: *The Man From Highbelow.* I was stunned. What Guy had told me was nothing compared to what I found. Having lived with the material for decades, he would not have been able to anticipate the intensity I felt upon seeing the collection. Besides, he is not a scholar; Guy is an artist, a master craftsman, not a writer. What pleased me most, perhaps, was that my grandfather had been so organized. It was almost as if he had prepared the files just for me! That's how I felt; for they had been sitting there for years without a single person perusing them.

It didn't take long before I realized that there was no way I would be able to input all the material in three weeks. When I asked Guy how he felt about my having the files shipped home so I could work on them over a period of months he was, understandably, adamant about keeping everything inside the barn; if something happened to them, that was it. Then I asked if it would be alright to take the files to a copy shop, but he still wasn't too keen on that. After listening to his reasoning, I agreed and decided that I would somehow get a copy machine inside the barn so I could stand there as long as it took and use the space of the barn to properly organize, so as not to misplace any of the papers. I got out the *Yellow Pages*, and after just a few calls came upon a Canon distributor who proved to be my angel. He delivered a small yet perfect machine, picked it up twenty days later, and charged me $150 including paper and toner. His offer was truly generous, and I accepted the gift as a grant from God.

I spent six to ten hours a day inside that barn. If there had been a toilet, I would have slept there. I was in granddaughter/writer bliss. How many people have the opportunity in their short lives to feel the power of such discovery? Every cell of my being was focused on my grandfather while inside the barn. Time was irrelevant as past, present, and future mixed like paint on a palette. I gazed regularly at the hidden stacks of canvases that reside inside the cavities that Guy had built to house the paintings. He'd built a loft as well, and often I would walk up the ladder and stand there just to be closer to the paintings up top. They were alive, and I sensed that they were watching over me. They smiled down upon my busy hands as I made copies and input documents. They comforted me when I'd be struck by a truth and fall into sobs. My soul convened with Wolff's whenever I turned my attention toward the paintings. A kindred meeting occurred nightly as I intentionally shut off the machines and just sat there on the sheepskin rug feeling the energy inside that barn.

The last night in the barn I sat on one of his rugs sobbing. I had discovered a peaceful bliss amongst the paintings and his words and did not want to leave. I had felt safe and loved, and now I had to return to the outside world where the security of Grandpa was nowhere to be found. "Till death takes me to you once again," I pledged out loud, "I am yours."

▣ ▣ ▣

Iᴛ ɪs ɴᴏᴡ Sᴘʀɪɴɢ 2001. Having begun researching the life of Robert J. Wolff back when I could not even imagine a year 2001, the amazement I feel, now that this project is being professionally printed and bound, is huge. Though it has been a wondrous (and often very challenging) 15 years since my search began, it is time to push this baby out the door. It's been quite a journey. And I am ready to let it go. Grandpa, thank you for leaving the world a document of your remarkably intense and meaningful life. May we all be able to take in the blessing of the essence you left here on Earth, and may you be living a healthy and happy life away from the Land of Mortals. Perhaps someday I will join you in Highbelow. And if so, you, the mortal reader, can rest assured that I will, as the writer, return to tell the tale.

Note:

In the pages that follow, *The Man From Highbelow* is presented in the words used by Robert Wolff. The reader should know, though, that my involvement entailed editing of the manuscript. Please know that this was not an attempt to "improve" my grandfather's writing, but some editing was truly needed. As one example, in the original manuscript there are segments that go on for pages without a paragraph break. From an objective professional standpoint, the reader can be assured that I have edited only what was necessary.

THE MAN FROM HIGHBELOW

Preface

(June 1971)

Until recently, it was my understanding that my name was Robert J. Wolff, and that I was born sixty-five years ago in Chicago on July 27. My sense of personal identity was suddenly shattered one rainy day in March, just three months ago when I discovered the yellowed pages of an unfinished manuscript at the bottom of a small trunk full of old papers.

I do not know exactly what led me to look into this long abandoned storehouse. Perhaps it was boredom with the life of an old man, and the hope that he might find some kind of renewal in these forgotten efforts. Perhaps it was nothing more than the aimless curiosity of a man with nothing better to do on a dreary day. Whatever the cause, the effect was depressing. One by one, as I read these confused and fragmentary literary efforts of my youth, I became more and more exasperated with myself for having opened the trunk at all. I was about to stuff the offending papers back where they came from (I never throw anything away) when my eye was caught by a heavy sheaf of paper lying in the corner. My curiosity was revived by the impression that there was a thick packet of typewritten pages, constituting what seemed to be a manuscript of a certain density. Compared to the other pages, random bits of things started but never finished, this new discovery

1

offered some promise of at least a sustained and substantial effort. I hope you, the reader, will agree that what I found was worth preserving. As you will discover, the manuscript gives a fragmented account of a land called Highbelow. I do not recall writing the words you are about to read. However, I have been aware of a strange sense of familiarity with the people and events described, a kind of deja-vu, absurd yet believable. Since the first reading, I have been obsessed with breaking through the opacity of consciousness to an experience that lives somewhere deep in the back areas of my remembered life, which I know is there, and which I must reveal to myself, and eventually to you.

Meanwhile, read on. Perhaps by the time you have finished with the contents of the mysterious manuscript, I shall have broken the barrier that stands between me and the elusive memories that came to life with the words that follow.

PART I

My name is Anoth, and in the course of my 226-year life I have seen many strange things. I am known throughout the length and breadth of Highbelow as the Ailing One. I have shrunk from 200 feet to a mere 50. I am sick, almost to death, with the *Four Fatal Maladies*: *looking back with longing, looking forward with anxiety, looking up with humility,* and *looking down with pride.*

I am writing this in the loneliness of my room. I have had strange and harrowing experiences which I feel the utmost necessity to relate. But I write with two audiences in mind: my own Highbelovians, and the people of the strange land wherein my hopeless sickness began. The difficulty that confronts me is to make myself clear to both, and both clear to the other. And because my mind is befuddled with the jumble of contrasts between the two, and since each will refuse to believe the other's existence, so greatly do they differ, I find myself looking forward to a task that seems more than I am up to.

Besides, I am a very sick man; sick with *looking back with longing, looking forward with anxiety, looking up with humility,* and *looking down with pride.* Under these conditions, telling the truth will take the strongest force of will. Tragically, few in Highbelow will even read this, for a writer in this land is, above all men, required to be entirely well, that is, free from the *Four Fatal Maladies* from which I suffer so terribly.

But this question of writers I mean to deal with presently, for it is a question that presents one of the sharpest and most important points of contrast

3

between my people and the other strange race which I have discovered. However, it is likely that I shall shrink away into nothingness before I complete what here I am beginning. For you see, I am *looking forward with anxious longing* to the time when this arduous book shall be finished so I may *look upon it with pride* and lazy satisfaction, and that alone condemns me to two of the most viscous of the *Four Maladies*.

However, I promise to summon up all the courage that my poor shrinking frame possesses and to carry out in the face of all these seemingly hopeless obstacles the job to which I have set myself.

◻◻◻

IT WILL SEEM STRANGE to that race of tiny men that the average height of a man in Highbelow is 200 feet. I say average, for he varies all the way from ten feet to 400. There is a legend in Highbelovian annals of a man who grew to a height of 700 feet before he disappeared into the skies, into the afterlife that all good Highbelovians attain.

But a man, in order to grow tall, must be absolutely free of taint from the Four Fatal Maladies. Sickness, as it is known among those funny little men who call themselves mortals, and to whom I have referred as the cause of my downfall, is unknown to Highbelovians. Our lives are terminated either by shrinking down through the ground to what is known as our hell or by expanding to such a tall and noble height that we seem to make contact with an all-powerful substance which lifts us into the unknown that is the Highbelovian heaven.

It is difficult to explain, this Highbelovian destiny. For destiny is the moving inevitable, and words are stationary, and the two are hostile. Those men who call themselves mortal are prone to honor the inquirer, the *looker-back* into the past and the *looker-forward* into the future. But alas, in Highbelow he is subject to a slow and deadly shrinkage. And the more he allows himself the idle luxury of selfish reflection, the smaller he gets. Yes, and the more he writes in this vein the smaller he gets until he vanishes from the face of the earth.

But I am getting ahead of myself, forgetting that half of my audience (I should say the whole of it perhaps, for I can only count on a few sick Highbelovians as readers) is totally unacquainted with the way in which the Highbelovians are constituted.

Let it be said then, that though we are many times as big as mortals, our bodies are built in every way the same. Our parts are identical—same bones, same red blood, same respiration, the same heartbeats, the same brain and body structure.

Yet, so are we born that no sooner are we out of our mother's womb, we seem to grasp the nature of things. And I believe that it is this quality that frees us from bodily decay, the wretched and fatal sickness to which the mortals are subject.

However, in place of bodily diseases, we are subject to diseases of the spirit, so to speak, which affect our lives as surely and fatally as actual decay of the body. For as I have said, our bodies shrink or expand according to the condition of our outlook on life.

To begin with, we are born with what would be known to Highbelovians if they stopped to consider it, as a perfect outlook. Free as we are from knowledge of our perfection, we grow at a tremendous rate until 25 years or so. Each Highbelovian, no matter what his fate may be in later years, lives a perfectly healthy life for the first 25 years. He is entirely unconscious of his perfect condition and consequently, does not try to better it. For if he were aware, he would naturally grow sick because he would not know when to leave well enough alone. Instead, he is free from worrying about what lies ahead, simply because he does not know that a future exists. That is, he is free from that *Malady* known as *looking forward with anxiety*.

On the other hand, the babe is blessed with the good sense to deny the existence of a past outside of what direct connection it has with his present problems. That is, he learns readily from experience without losing sight of the fact that the past has no existence whatsoever, and without being snared by the absurd idea of a time when he was better off than he happens to be at the present. He knows without realizing it (for the realization would be a latent wisdom, which is indeed a sickness) that memory makes things seem real which actually have no reality. Thus, he is free from the second *Fatal Malady* known as *looking back with longing*.

As for the other two *Maladies* which complete the scope of Highbelovian sicknesses, the child also has no knowledge of them. Although his growth is rapid, reaching 200 feet by his 25th year, he has no feeling of superiority over those of his older fellows who might be smaller than he. And it is not unusual to see a babe of 20 towering over his father of 150 for the obvious reason that the son's innocence keeps him from *looking up* to his father *with humility*. Few fathers, though, escape *looking down* on the thing they have bred from their own tissue; and in looking down, they immediately fall victim to *looking down with pride*, and begin rapid shrinkage. Thus, while a child is in his or her most rapid growth period, it is not uncommon for a father to begin a period of concentrated shrinkage. It is one of the snares of fatherhood.

Neither is the child subject to *looking up with humility*, for he has no fear of his elders. No Highbelovian parent, no matter how small he may be, (though no woman would have a man under 100 feet) could be stricken with so great a sense of superiority as to bully the child without shrinking at an instant's notice into sudden nothingness.

In this way, you see, the ebb and flow of a Highbelovian's life is bound in the *Four Fatal Maladies*. He will shrink in proportion to the amount of subjection to them and grow indefinitely as he remains free from them. And that, in short, is doom or salvation in Highbelow.

◻◻◻

Parent and Child and Early Life

THE HOUSE IN WHICH I was born was one of the most spacious in Highbelow. Three stories high, it was square in shape with no external decoration, save square openings for the windows. One could tell at a glance that the inhabitants were healthy simply because each story was a good 300 feet high, while the perfect simplicity of the exterior further showed that the builders were altogether free from *looking down with pride*. For on the houses of less healthy Highbelovians one would find embellishments here and there which were obviously put there out of conceit. These decorative conceits are noticeable to all Highbelovians no matter how insignificant or unpretentious the owner has tried to make them. Thus, when people pass a house which has a fine, simple exterior, save for the damning evidence of a gargoyle rising surreptitiously from a corner of the roof, they know that the inhabitants are not as healthy as they might be. But no mention is ever made of these evident failings, for as soon as they are noticed people immediately put them out of their minds, guarding themselves as they do with the instinct they are born with to steer clear of that feeling of superiority which might tempt the healthy ones to look patronizingly on their less fortunate, ailing fellows.

So you see, in Highbelow a man cannot lord it over his fellow man, for no matter how brave a front he may be able to put forward, the moment he begins the act of lording it over, he begins shrinking so that his falseness and pretense are at once obvious to all. And so finding himself shrinking, he will see the futility of his false pride and right himself again to the point where his outlook is once again healthy. Sometimes, however, the shrinking so frightens a man that he is unable to escape the sense of inferiority which follows and before he can save himself he has shrunk into nothingness and death.

But I was describing the house I was born in, and here I find myself talking of things which must be reserved for special sections such as architecture and art and Highbelovian death. But I am so overcome with *looking forward* to getting this job over with that I am letting myself cross the bridge before I get there, which has contributed no little shrinkage to my already fastly shrinking body. Since I have started writing this, I have lost no less than two inches. I can only hope that I will be preserved until I have had my full say, though I feel that to be highly improbable. Two inches are already lost after but a few hundred words. And I intend to write thousands. The outlook is indeed dark for me and for those of my readers who would like to hear the whole of my tale.

My father was 300 feet when I was born, one of the tallest men in Highbelow. From birth he had grown without interruption, save for several slight setbacks which but one man in all Highbelovian history has been able to escape. After all, Highbelovians are human, and pride and humility, conceit and anxiety, idle, longing and all the little ailments of the spirit to which men are subject are just as apt to take hold of a Highbelovian as anyone else. Yet, so powerful is the foundation of innocence at birth that they are capable, luck being with them, of having no experience with the *Maladies* whatsoever. This, of course, is rare.

The home into which I was born was a happy one, that is, a healthy one. My grandfather had already taken leave of us before my birth, having been lifted into the skies after a fine healthy life of 300 years and 450 feet. I remember the day my father gave in to the temptation to boast about his father. We were walking together in the street, my father towering some hundred feet above me, for I was but 15 years old. Suddenly I noticed him perceptively shrinking, an occurrence which was new to me, for I had never, in all my short life, seen him do anything other than grow tall, so noble and innocent and healthy was his life among us.

Having no knowledge of the effect of the *Maladies*, being yet less than 25 years of age, I could only guess that something was momentarily wrong with my father. Then he began to speak, giving word to the thoughts that had caused the shrinkage. He told me of his father who had grown taller than any man in the memory of anyone then living in Highbelow. At the instant of this utterance from his 300 feet, I noticed him to shrink by 20. I paid no attention, feeling neither one way nor the other regarding his welfare. For in Highbelow people instinctively attend to no one's ailments but their own, even if the ailing one is one's own parent. But after my father had uttered this prideful reflection, he ceased to give thought to it. In fact, so courageous and healthy a man was he that the 20 feet shrinkage bothered him not at all, and before the day was out he was back to his normal height.

However, if the relation of parent and child had been anything but what it was in Highbelow, the results of this incident might have been fatal both to my father and to myself. For if we had had that sense of filial/parental duty which makes leeches out of father and son in the Land of Mortals, we would have both been so foolishly concerned with each other's private thoughts and problems that we would have started a relationship that could not end in anything but a shrinking death for both. A mortal son in this instance would have worried himself sick wondering what the neighbors would think. A mortal father would have become upset imagining that his son had lost respect for him, and feared that the boy was frightened for his elder's life. They both would have ended up with a bad case of *looking forward with anxiety, looking down with pride*, and *looking up with humility*.

But you see, as it was, I was not concerned with my father's life, knowing instinctively that he could best take care of himself. And my father, on his part, did not worry that the slip he had made in pridefully mentioning his father would have any bad effect on me, knowing me for a true Highbelovian son who minded his own business. And so, free from the burden of carrying my mind's problems along with his own, he was able in short order to correct himself of his momentary indisposition.

My father's name was Sornodigam, and it was by that title that I always called him; for "Father" and "Mother" are unknown in Highbelow as salutatory words. I have no memory of ever placing my father above anyone in Highbelow just because he was my father. For you see, that heritage of common discernment, which is innate in all Highbelovians from birth, made it plain to me the moment I was able to see that the man who inhabited the house I was born into was in no way or manner different from the other men who lived in other houses. I took no special pride in my father; for you see, he was a very healthy man and failed to make me feel in any way obligated to him for having engendered me. In fact, it was some years before I even learned that he was my father, and when he did make that fact known to me, he did it in such a casual way that he might have been explaining that five and five make ten.

I remember distinctly the day he approached me on this subject. I was ten years old and at the moment in question was occupied with making a chair for my sleeping room. I was working in the large, airy room that had been set aside for me to teach myself to make useful things. My father entered and greeted me. "Anoth, with what are you occupied?"

"Sornodigam, I am making a chair."

I showed him what I had done, and he offered his opinion, what he thought was done well, and what was badly wrought. I listened to all he had to say and of course his remarks were so obviously based upon a broader experience of carpentry than was mine that I set about immediately to correct the parts that were badly put together. For you see, I had no wish out of childish perversity, as mortal children seem to be cursed with, to contradict my father's advice simply for the sake of self-assertion. I had never been made to feel inferior just because of my smaller stature and fewer years, or because he was my father. For a father who does this usually makes a child feel smaller, younger, and more erring than he really is and the child, sensing the injustice of his situation, is inclined to over self-assertion in the attempt to bring himself back to his just level.

And so, on this day, after my father had spoken to me about my work, I immediately set myself to the job of finishing the chair. My father stood above me while I worked. And I worked well, for I could feel that he was considering my work for what it was, rather than as the special work of his particular son, which would have inspired me with so great a desire to satisfy his selfish pride that I would have bungled in the heat of my anxiety to please.

As it was, I was progressing well with the chair when my father said, "Anoth, do you know how you came into the world?"

I answered him, "No, Sornodigam, I do not."

And it was true; I did not know, nor had I ever had any suspicion or curiosity about the phenomenon of my being here. For during my ten years of life, I had been so busy learning the business of living, so eager to scotch the present for what it was worth, that I had no time for day-dreaming of any sort. The reason for this is that in Highbelow, there are no forms of literature for children such as fairy tales to paint in their imaginations a world that does not exist, tales which make their dissatisfaction with the one they live in all the keener. Nor were there any stage plays or moving shadow pictures to which mortals foolishly send their children which represent this world as something entirely different from what it really is, thus perverting their knowledge of it just as that knowledge is naturally budding. Nor did my father, or mother for that matter, ever speak to me of my life in terms of theirs, which would have made me strive to be a man that I was not and would have forced me to apply their solutions to my problems, which is every man's necessity to settle for himself.

No, there was nothing in all my youth to make me feel that I was anyone but myself, or that my surroundings were anything but what they were. And so it naturally followed that my life was real and full and so taken up with the actualities as they presented themselves each day that I had no time for the dreaming that corrodes the lives of mortal children, wherein they try to settle in their minds just which one of all their dream men they are and which one they ought to try to imitate. Nor had I time for idle speculation on things that I had no knowledge of, such as how I had come into this world.

Thus, when my father asked me this question I was not over eager to hear it, because I had no pent-up curiosity about it inasmuch as the past had no existence for me, save what experiences I could take out of it for present usage. As it was, the fact of my birth had no apparent connection with the chair I was making, so the subject seemed irrelevant, that is, uninteresting.

My father's reason for bringing up this subject is only clear to me now, and it proves to me the great wisdom of the man. My memory of the blundering mortal fathers with whom I came into contact during my visit to their land makes my own father's common sense, and all Highbelovian fathers' common sense for that matter, stand out by contrast as something miraculous. And yet, was any Highbelovian to consider his action in this respect toward his sons, he would count it all in the day's work and turn from me in disgust for making a mountain out of a mole hill. But they, lucky people, are not cursed like me with the memory of men who make Highbelovians stand out like gods in contrast. Yes, I am cursed, cursed for that regrettable visit I made to the mortals' land. For I indeed feel like a god when I think of myself in relation to those people. I, oh horrible fate, can feel myself slowly shrinking. I can feel it in my bones and tissues and I am inspired with fear. For I am *looking back with longing* to those days when I was healthy, *looking forward with anxiety* to my shrinking death, *looking down with pride* on the mortals, and *looking up with humility* to my own Highbelovians. Woe is me!

But I must control the agony in which the *Four Fatal Maladies* grip me and get on with my writings; for if I don't, I shall not live out many more pages.

Where was I? Oh yes, the reason for my father's mention of the manner in which I came into the world. You see, I was very young. Ten years, that is all, fifteen years off from Highbelovian puberty, the time when I'd look upon a woman with the desire of a man. (Puberty in Highbelow is not reached until boys or girls are 25 years of age, being by that time ripe in experience, wise in the mind, and useful to themselves and others.)

Like other Highbelovian fathers who concern themselves with their sons only in matters they cannot learn for themselves, my father realized that just as you could not expect a hungry man to analyze the chemical ingredients of a side of beef, neither could you expect a boy just turning man to understand the facts that underlain his newly discovered desires. In Highbelow, it is usual for a lad turning 25 to begin his first period of shrinkage. But so well has he lived, so full is his maturity, that his mind is prepared to grasp the significance of the setback he is undergoing. And with this understanding of life well tucked away in his mind, he is not bowled over at the first real battle with it. For the shrinkage appears as natural, and he is not at all frightened at his predicament, and so he is able to pass it off lightly and come out of it none the worse for the experience.

My father realized that I was better equipped at ten to receive the knowledge of conception and birth than I would be at 25. And so he related to me in detail the manner in which men and women mate and the fact that they find good pleasure in it and that the man sends his seed into the woman where it meets and mixes with her seed, which forms within her and grows into the body of the child, to which she eventually gives birth through the same portal through which she received the seed from the man. The woman, my father then told me, was known as "mother" of the child, and the man as "father." I remembered the names "mother" and "father" as purely biological references to Sornodigam and Tinedra. And my father told me that in a scientific way I was what is known as his "son." Likewise, did I catalogue that word "son" in my mind as a scientific term for me who was rightly called and known as Anoth.

In this way, I grew up with a fine objective knowledge of the forces that later would become a part of my life. And when those forces finally entered into me, I knew them for what they were and I was not carried away by them. I never developed evil or perverse thoughts on the matter, for these arise out of ignorance, and I was well stocked with the sanity of knowledge.

And so I grew up taking the natural physical relationship of men and women as a matter of course, just as I would expect them to eat and drink.

The idea of a woman being a mother, a man a father, or a boy a son, I took as a very simple fact that people did not make much of. My mother was to me an upright woman whose name was Tinedra. I was attached to her not because I had been taught to deify her motherhood, but because I actually liked her.

I cannot make this point too plain; for it is the basis of the Highbelovian parent/child relationship. The child has two friends, a man and a woman in whose house he lives and who support him until he is able to support himself. He feels not in the least indebted to them; for he knows they brought him into the world to see him through while he is learning the ways of life. He feels no obligation to like them and consequently considers them rationally for the man and woman they really are. Because very little *looking forward, backward, up* or *down* exists, people expect nothing — they simply take what they get. Thus a child is not to his parents what he should or should not be, but what he is. They leave the making of his life to him for better or for worse. A son who turns out well and healthy is welcome to live among his parents. But one who turns out to be unhealthy is subject to his own fate which replaces the parental reprimand with due shrinkage and, if he is incorrigible, with ultimate obliteration.

Thus, I lived in perfect harmony with my parents until puberty. My mother was tall like my father and a model of good health. Only at my birth do I remember her shrinking. Escaping this is rare, however, for it is more natural than at any other time of life for a mother to be seized with the impulse for complete possession of the thing to which she has given birth. It takes a woman of the greatest health to rightly understand that that which has been part of her body for so long, and which has been torn from her womb under the greatest pain, is no longer part of her and is beginning an individualized existence.

Although my mother did not conduct herself perfectly, she stood up to the temptation of calling herself a "mother." However, the very thought of possessing another human, regardless of the fact that she did not put the thought into words, brought about a shrinkage of some 30 feet. (*Looking down with prepossession* is a form of *looking down with pride*.) But because she was healthy to begin with, standing at the normal 100 feet, she immediately righted herself, and thereafter looked upon me solely as a man called "Anoth," one who needed her care in certain details of life.

My mother's case, of course, is an exemplary one. For she was back to normal before leaving bed, which was only an hour or so after giving birth. I have known more than one case in Highbelow of a mother who became so hysterically insistent that the child, although already out of her womb, still belonged to her that she shrank away immediately into nothingness and death — into hell. And I have seen the husbands of such women, upon hearing of their horrible death, shrug their shoulders and remark that the child is better off without any woman to look after him than to be babied into the realization that a woman gave birth to him and thus his every attendance could be expected, even those that the child ought rightly enough do for himself.

And so it happens that in Highbelow the main worry of the husband (and this worry is often followed by shrinkage, due to *looking forward with anxiety*) occurs when his wife is brought to bed with child. I say this here for the benefit of my mortal friends. For it was the worry of the mortal parents as to the mother's physical welfare that surprised me to no end. For in Highbelow there is no reason to fear the death of the mother from a mere physical breakdown, but rather from a complete collapse of her moral health.

So, far my mortal readers will have undoubtedly gotten the impression that the Highbelovians are an extremely stern race. In comparison to them, this impression is indeed correct. But they are really only stern with themselves; each individual makes the most of his own life on earth and lets his fellow men do what they will. For no matter what they do, there is no earthly use in correcting them. Because when they fall into bad ways, and thus are ill, it is only they who can help themselves. As soon as they turn to others, they simply add another setback to their falling health. Thus, no one need be stern with anyone else; a Highbelovian's greatest necessity to himself, as a man in his own right and as a member of a community, is to see that he keeps his own health in good order. Therefore, men and women pay no attention to ailing ones, but will have only to do with healthy people with whom they can have rational and happy intercourse.

But this sternness with one's self of which I speak is always doubled in a house where a birth is impending. It is more a matter of impulse than of deliberation, for to deliberately set out to strengthen one's backbone is certainly a form of acknowledging, rather than of dispersing, fear. The Highbelovian woman who finds herself with child will immediately approach her husband with the information. If she is as healthy as was my mother, she will make her condition known to him in a precisely matter-of-fact way and the husband, if he is equally as healthy, will take what she tells him in the same spirit. Should he be smitten with the impulse to think of himself as someone different than he was before he knew of his fatherhood, he will naturally shrink some. The germ of *looking down with prepossession* and *pride* will begin its work within him, and if his general health is not sound the germ will make inroads. A serious affliction might then ensue.

The mother, for her part, is even more susceptible to shrinkage at this time. For if she tells her husband about her pregnancy in a way as to imply that she considers herself more important than she was before, she will be running right into trouble. She will begin a period of shrinkage that will keep up until she has purged herself of the notion that she should be complimented for the creation of something with which she, actually, had nothing to do. For when she rightly understands that the new life within her is part of a natural course of events, and as such cannot be held up as anything she has fashioned by her own hand and out of her own mind, then she will assume the proper role of motherhood and prosper in health.

It is by a sort of instinct that Highbelovian fathers and mothers understand the exigency that they must rise to when a child of their own blood is being brought into the world. There is no reference made between them to their being mother and father as well as husband and wife. A woman will walk about the streets in the last stages of pregnancy without it even occurring to her that she is different from the people all about her. And if passersby notice her condition they, for their part (if they are healthy), will only see a woman who is soon to give birth to a child, not a woman to be censored for shameless exposure. Nor would a healthy Highbelovian treat her with wonder and awe, as though childbirth was something miraculous, as though any ten-year-old could not thoroughly explain the whole matter. What is known to my tiny mortal friends as the miracle of motherhood is no more astonishing to Highbelovians than the growth of a beet root. Consequently, it is easy to understand that the women in Highbelow are uncommonly interesting individuals. Their position as mothers of boys makes no impression on the men whatsoever. As a result, the women do more original things than produce children in order to call up a response in their men.

In recalling my own babyhood I am at once confronted with one of the most striking differences between the Highbelovian conception of man and the ideas that mortals have about themselves. To begin with, a Highbelovian baby is looked upon with the utmost respect as soon as it is born. The fact of his or her own helplessness in regard to the rudimentary necessities of life has no bearing on the more important qualities, as Highbelovians see it, with which he or she is blessed. The mother is not prejudiced in any way against the child for his natural inability to attend himself. She washes him until he has learned to wash himself. She feeds him and diapers him, and performs all the unpleasant duties that every mother in the animal kingdom is obliged to perform for her young.

But the Highbelovian infant is looked upon as an important member of the community because of his heritage of perfect health, being absolutely free from the *Four Fatal Maladies* and, what is more important, from the possibility of being contaminated by others. He is, in fact, a purifier of any home into which he is born whose inhabitants are in the least way ailing. He brings the moral strength of the indomitable, the incorruptible. Men and women who have been known to be ailing with anxiety about each other, who have been sick with competitive pride and consequent haggling and quarreling, who have been under the curse of the *Four Fatal Maladies* in one form or another, suddenly were restored to disinterestedness and normal health the moment a babe was born among them. The babe's noble indifference to the pettiness of the sick seems to awaken them to a sense of their own foolishness, and in the face of such unwavering normality, their spirits strengthen. They seem to catch the perfect outlook of the child who has none of *looking forward with anxiety*, or *looking back with longing, looking up with humility*, or *looking down with pride*.

So when you find a mother who has been sick with berating her husband for not giving her as much attention as when they began living together, or when you find a husband who has been constantly accusing his wife of interfering in one way or another with the progress of his own life—when you find two people like this, hopelessly shrinking from sickness, suddenly finding themselves the mother and father of a child possessing all the qualities that their own sickness is eating away in themselves, a child impregnably entrenched behind his own unassailable health, then that man and woman will look at each other and laugh. From that moment on, they will follow the noble example of their babe who demonstrates the supreme faculty of minding his own business.

The notion among the mortals that an infant wouldn't be worth the trouble of its keep if the parents did not have the consolation of looking forward to its someday growing into an adult duplication of the parents themselves, is a notion unheard of in Highbelow. In the first place, the child is considered entirely in the light of what he is rather than what he will be someday. And, whereas mortal parents make out of the babe a plaything for themselves until he is ripe to learn their way of mind, Highbelovian parents take the child seriously to begin with, conceding him the capacity for a full feeling for life the moment he is born. The Highbelovian infant has a right to his own likes and dislikes. For instance, if friends of the parents pay them a visit, no matter how dear to the parents these friends might be, there is no effort made on the part of anyone to induce the babe to be amiable to the visitors if he happens to make it plain that he does not feel the same way about them as do his parents. And should the child behave badly before the visitors, he is not punished or censored, for all parties realize that he has no other way of expressing his adverse opinion.

The formula that Highbelovian parents generally follow in guiding the behavior of an infant is quite simple. No doubts ever enter their minds that the babe is not possessed from birth with normal perception and common discernment. They gladly realize that the newcomer is free from the perversions of outlook that might arise from the prejudices with which older men are liable to be infected, rating one man as better than another for purely subjective reasons which have no bearing on the true merits of the man in question. Parents know that it will do no good to try to persuade the child that his father is better than other men or that his mother is better than other women simply because circumstances have led them to live under the same roof. They know that the child is above bowing to such an influence, for his outlook is incorruptibly perfect.

As a result of this foregone conviction, no time is wasted. The focus remains on teaching the child the essentials of human behavior by impressing upon him that his first duty in life is to nobody other than himself. Thus, the first words he is taught are "food," "drink," "water," and "bowels." By speaking these essentials, the infant is saved the trouble of making himself uncomfortable, for his stronger and more adept elders will not simply watch the babe crying himself sick; they will honor his spoken needs. And when these words are learned, and the child associates them with the prime physical exigencies of life, the parents are pleased.

All of this cannot but call up in mind a certain father I knew during my visit to the mortal's land whom I found one day trying with all his heart and soul to make his infant child repeat the word, "Papa." The child was screaming and twisting in his bed, nearly mad with the discomfort of wetting himself. And the father took it into his head that the babe was a funny little beast who might learn in time but was in his present state a bawling idiot. Now, a Highbelovian father, being quite prideless about the infant, would have understood the necessity of the moment, which was relieving the child of his discomfort and teaching him a word that might be of some use when next he wanted to make known that he felt the need to urinate. But evidently, the mortal father in question was more concerned with himself as a father, and with an acknowledgment of that quite commonplace fact from his son, than he was in the immediate welfare of the child. Yet this incident is only one of thousands which confronted me in the mortals' land and made me wonder how such a backward people could go on in this manner and still survive.

When it comes to infants, the Highbelovian method of procedure is so to the point that it is rare that a child, in the hands of able and healthy parents, is not able to convey his premonitions of bodily necessities by means of definite and meaningful sound before he is many months old. To mortal parents who are still diapering a child after he has been taught that its parents are the two greatest people in the world, the development of the Highbelovian infant will seem miraculously rapid. Yet it stands to reason that the infant whose first and only association with a definite word with a definite perception rests in the word, "Papa" will stay far behind the one who is taught from the start only words that have some definite bearing on his own urgent welfare.

Of course you who are mortals cannot imagine how utterly tedious it is to record what, to my Highbelovian outlook, is all very simple and commonplace. For the manners and habits of thought such as I am explaining here are part of a man's daily life, and he carries on with them without paying them any mind. And so my making much of the fact that people make no use of the word "Mother" in Highbelow seems as silly to me as it would seem to a mortal to make out that his daily use of that word is something extraordinary. So, to bear up with my subject at all I am forced to keep constantly in mind that such a race as mortals exists and that to them the perfectly simple behavior of the Highbelovian appears very odd. This very necessity, of keeping my strange friends in mind, results in a coincidental stream of contempt, which only speeds up the infectious course of my fatal illness and shortens my days, which are already sadly numbered.

But I must go on.

By the time I was five years-old and in full command of our language, I was taking a respectable part in the life of our home. At forty feet tall, I had grown well, though my small stature made me feel in no way less an individual than my parents who were some five times taller. It wasn't until the day I entered the Land of Mortals that I even considered the dignity of my childhood position in my parents' house, and then it was only brought to mind by the shocking subordination there of every aspect of a child's life to the soaring superiority of his elders.

I could hardly believe my eyes when once, for example, I was present at a gathering of people at a prominent gentleman's home (held on the lawn, because of my comparatively large stature) and at meal time the two children of the house were commanded to take themselves to their own place for dining. Astonished, I watched them eat alone as everyone, including the children, accepted the conclusion that the younger ones were not developed enough to conduct themselves as their elders did. Of course, the children, understanding that naughtiness was expected of them, never refrained from being naughty, but waited instead until they were caught and forcibly stopped from behaving badly. Because their whole method of approach was based on the premise that the children were bad and barbarous and perverse to begin with, the parents encouraged this state of mind.

You who are mortals have the example of the lady who asks the little boy, "Are you a good boy my little man?" Of course the child's answer is affirmative, although he does not in his heart believe it, having been questioned too often on the subject and finally coming to the conclusion that he'd be something quite extraordinary if he was a good boy. He cannot help but gather from the nature of the silly question that whoever is asking it strongly suspects that he is not a good boy. And if indeed he was a good boy answering, "Yes, I am a good boy," it would only be due to his remarkable ability to overcome his natural badness, which then would deserve a compliment that comes in the form of a patronizing pat on the head.

It was all very different in my own home. As far back as I can remember, even as a babe in the crib, I never received a patronizing word from any adult person who came near me. Until I was able to walk I was, of course, carried about, but this took place only when there was a real occasion to move me from one place to another. I was never picked up to satisfy my elders' need to feel big, or so they could take pride in the fact that I was entirely dependent upon them. I grew out of my babyhood with no memory of being tossed about in the air with my father's powerful hands. Nor do I recall being carried around simply for my mother's amusement in front of her lady friends. But I saw these things happen to babies in the mortals' land. And I never wondered that the children there grow up without ever really getting out of their systems the sensation of those big powerful hands, without ever ridding themselves of the feeling that anyone old enough to be their mother or father will always have the right to toss them about in the air, if not in the actual sense, at least in every other matter that touches their lives.

Of course, it follows that I grew out of babyhood and into childhood without a trace of shyness toward those who were older and bigger than myself. At the age of five I had no fear of anyone. I sat at the table with my elders at mealtime. I listened with intelligence to what they had to say, and when I wanted to make a remark of my own, relevant to the thing being discussed, I was listened to with ordinary attention, not with the excess of attention that some parents give as though they were expecting something remarkable to emerge from the mouth of their own creation, or with too little attention, as though the child was bound to say something ridiculous, being that the source was so much younger than they and therefore less wise.

In regard to this, it struck me as quite funny that the mortals who, one and all, being grievously stricken with *looking forward with anxiety*, considered the advance of years a calamity, something to be ashamed of, and thus tried to console their vanity with the idea that wisdom goes with age. Whether they were really wise or not, they considered old people to be wise. And the old people grudgingly accepted this regard for their assumed wisdom in place of the more desirable attention that their youth at one time drew. It seems so queer a compromise to me who, as a Highbelovian, is accustomed to people who live for hundreds of years without ever giving so much as a thought to what they are or what they will be or how they will be regarded by people in the future in contrast to what people thought of them in the past. Progress and learning appear as natural to every individual as it goes on in him day by day. There is nothing that would make a man live empty days grinding away at a job that means nothing to him but the fruits of which mean everything. For if he likes not what he is doing, what does he have after it is done? The doing is all that actually is part of him, while the having-done is a thing removed, a thing finished and not demanding of him anything but his idle admiration and satisfaction.

You must see how all this is intimately bound up in the state of complete freedom from *looking forward with anxiety*, for that sickness condemns a man to looking away from what he is doing and so takes all the reality out of life. Again, among the mortals I failed to find but a few who were not inextricably caught in the meshes of this malady, the only ones free of the malady were, ironically enough, men who did no work of any sort, who were poor or rich to the point of complete indifference as to what they did with their lives. And it seemed strange to me that the men with this indifference about the future in Highbelow should be among the most useful in the community, while in the mortals' land they are quite the most useless.

But to get back to the matter of children—as I said, I reached the age of five without a trace of shyness toward my elders. But neither was I overly bold amidst them. For extreme shyness and extreme boldness in a child come from the same source. Both are the result of an overbearing attitude on the part of the adults. The shyness is a retreat from this attitude, and the boldness protests against it. In both cases, the child has shut himself off from the possibility of honest communication with his elders, and the natural result is a complete estrangement and a situation where understanding between them is impossible. As a consequence, in the Land of Mortals each generation as it comes forth sees life in a different way, and this difference of outlook leaves the one generation a stranger to its predecessor.

But that is wrong. For no matter what the changes may be from time to time, the individual has to adjust, the parent no less than the child. There is no foundation to the argument that as the child is meeting his first adjustment, the parents have already gotten so accustomed to their own generation that they find it too difficult to adjust to the new order. A child has the task of learning what adjustment even is, while the parents are already experienced in this and simply have to give a new twist to what they have already learned. No, it is not the differences in outlook that make a mother in the Land of Mortals a stranger to her daughter, but rather, the fact that she has never allowed the daughter to feel as much a woman as she. And the daughter, as a consequence, becomes uncommunicative either out of shyness for the illusion of superiority that the mother has created around herself, or out of protest against the failure of her mother to look upon her daughter as mature.

As it was, I enjoyed my parents tremendously. But now that I look back, I see my fondness for them had a rational base. I was inclined to like them mainly because they gave no indication of anxiety over the quality of my feeling for them, and because they allowed me the full privacy of my own feelings. You see, it is not in the nature of the true Highbelovian to qualify his relationship to this or that person. When he likes a person, they get along and naturally they spend time together. And when he does not like a person he sees very little of him. But where he differs in this respect to the mortals is that he is free from the sort of mindedness which would have him decide before he has had any actual contact or experience with a person. Judgment is never passed based upon physical impulse, social position, or forgathered reports of the admirable things he is accomplishing in his life. When one meets another for the first time, there is no prejudice one way or the other. Because in Highbelow, the individual, by reason of a common birthright, realizes that his reputation contributes nothing to his manner of relating one man to the other.

Thus, there are no injurious relationships in Highbelow where two people rate each other as good friends for reasons which have come up from outside of their own intercourse, such as out of pride for each other's reputations or positions in the society, or out of fear for them or worship of them. Thus, you will never find two people who are reputed to like each other, talking maliciously behind the other's back. When you see two people associating together, even if they are husband and wife, you know that they are congenial from the bottom of their hearts.

Of course, you can imagine how strange it seemed to me in the Land of Mortals, where so much was written about brotherly love, where friendship and love were abundantly eulogized. You can imagine how amazed I was at every turn to find each distrusting the other to such an extent that they were no more able to communicate honestly with each other than the children I have spoken of were able to communicate honestly with their parents. It was that pretense of superiority, that anxiety on the part of each one to appear more impressive than the next fellow, that cut off one man from another exactly as it cut off parent from child. Truly was every mortal man and woman hopelessly stricken with *looking down with pride*. And yet they all managed to survive. Yet, so great is the confusion of their innermost values that those who are most sorely stricken manage to live the longest in many cases. But this is because the mortal society is constructed so as to be congenial to their perversities, and even encouraging to them, and as a consequence only the most perverse can gain the wealth that will furnish the comforts and care to preserve their bodies into what to them is an old age. You see how entirely the reverse of this is the state of affairs in Highbelow. Whereas a man would not get far in the mortal's land without *looking down with pride*, in Highbelow those men live longest who keep themselves most free from it. But we in Highbelow need not worry about the decay of our bodies and therefore are not driven to such unhealthy means to preserve them.

And so I grew well and quickly midst the happy surroundings in which I lived. I had many friends among the boys of the neighborhood. We played at games, that is true, and we played hard. And yet we had no dominant idea of playing for the sole sake of beating out the other fellow and asserting ourselves over and above our friends. We found no example of this spirit anywhere in the society in which we were born and, hence, had no idea of this. I can safely say that a boy from Highbelow, were he to be suddenly transferred to a mortal home and told in the usual manner by the father of the house to glorify the family and himself by beating out the other boys, he would not know what to do. For there is none of that kind of early training in Highbelow which grooms a child from the crib to undertake everything better than the other fellow. If this were so, the homes would be turning out young men whose only urge to do anything at all would be in the desire to excel, the actual endeavor itself making little difference outside of its propensity to attract attention. Thus, Highbelovian children grow up without confusion about what they like to do for its own sake and what they may think they like to do for its own sake, but which really means to them little more than a road to glory.

Among my childhood friends, our games never meant anything like this, for lacking as we were in competitive pride we found our sole enjoyment in playing to a common standard of excellence. Our goal was to develop our skill up to this standard which, when reached, gave us an individual satisfaction that had nothing to do with the better or worse accomplishments of our friends. The idea that reigns in the mortals' land of competition being the soul of achievement tends to turn out children who are either unbearably blown up over a personal victory or hopelessly discouraged and broken over a personal defeat. As a consequence, the standard of excellence there is so low that were a Highbelovian to observe it he would become so conscious of his enormous advancement over the mortals that he would suddenly become stricken with *looking down with pride* (like me!).

Consider, for example, the sport of jumping of which we in Highbelow have an equivalent. The mortal can barely jump his own height, while the ordinary standard, which every young man in Highbelow attains, is five times his own height. For when a Highbelovian jumps he is scot-free of any dragging apprehension that the next fellow might make a better jump, or that he will disappoint anyone if he does not make a good jump, or that he will be censored and *looked down upon* if he doesn't live up to everyone's expectations of the extent of his prowess, or that a good performance will draw an overbearing avalanche of praise. If we burdened ourselves with these fearful thoughts, no matter what line of endeavor we were pursuing, we would shrink so rapidly that we would become too small to take our places among our fellows. And it is this impulse in us that makes us, even as children (I should say even more so as children), do everything that we undertake simply for the doing.

Additionally, intellectual standards are what would seem inconceivably vast to mortal men. As a child of ten I was able to multiply with but an instant's thought three numbers of six ciphers each. Of course, at the time I had no idea that I was doing anything extraordinary, for the presence of even a spark of reflective pride in the act would have upset the perfect order of my mind, crowding out the natural processes of thought. For one part pride takes up the same room in the rational thought process as a million times its equivalent in disinterested reasoning. So when you consider the amount of personal pride that this spirit of mortal competition brings into any kind of endeavor you can imagine how little room there is left for the true function of the mind. In Highbelow it is different. Men think here without thinking of themselves, and consequently reach heights of thought undreamed of in the Land of Mortals.

The woeful condition of my present health cannot be attributed to any inadequacies in my early life. My parents fostered my curiosities and gave impetus to every inquiry I made into the nature of anything that puzzled me. They allowed nothing that once had awakened my inquisitiveness to remain a mystery. For if the inherent curiosities of the Highbelovian child about the nature of the world into which he has been thrust are allowed to go unsatisfied, he will ultimately become careless and heedless of life. At twenty-five, he will first awaken to a dire need for a broad knowledge that will hold him above the storm that comes down upon him at that age. Without proper preparation, he would find himself stranded with no background to widen, no self-gathered knowledge to expand, no fullness of mind to hold his head above the forces that sweep down upon him. He would be conscious of his own weakness and of the strength of others. He would become anxious to learn, not of his own free will, to find at any cost the secret of his own strength. He would try to cram his head full of all the knowledge that he failed to discover during the natural growth of his childhood. His regrets for his lost years would consume him with *looking back with longing*. His anxiety to catch up with those whose development has been normal would fill him with *looking forward with anxiety*. He would feel that though he was to live forever he could hardly hope to know as much as his normal fellows. For when a man goes after knowledge simply to feed his pride, he becomes a real monster. Thus the afflicted one adds to his miseries the infection of *looking up with humility*, and this is enough to seal his doom.

Such a man is lucky to live to twenty-six. His lot is sadly reminiscent of the poor mortal children to whom education amounts to little more than a gesture of defense against a world of barren elders who honor the prestige of the learned rather than their learning, who deplore the ignominy of the un-learned rather than their lack of learning. What drudgery must the process of learning be, and what happiness of mind they must altogether miss.

One day when but a mere babe, I was seen in my crib to be giving a con-cerned and concentrated attention to the phenomenon of opening and clos-ing my hand. The act seemed to me, once I had discovered it, to be quite wonderful and at the same time awakened in me great awe. I came to a vague but overwhelming realization that the opening and shutting of the hand I held in front of my face was an act of my own doing. Through my consciousness swept the colossal meaning of my own will, the unbelievable wonder of ME. I lay back in my crib and held my hand before my eyes, and opened and shut it with reckless abandon, no longer a disinterested inquisi-tor into the phenomenon of my fingers. Had I been a mortal, I would have set up a tyranny of a dumb and unreasoning will over a marvelously delicate and complex mechanism. And not only that, so badly would I have con-fused the act of willing with the labor of creating that I would have added to the delight of controlling my finger joints the conceit that may have come from thinking I'd conceived and created them.

But I had attentive parents. My father, who had been watching me, noticed the change in attitude toward my fingers. He noticed my complete satisfaction with myself and how I had suddenly substituted a vacant pride for the spirit of discovery. He knew that I was shirking the taking of food for thought and he knew that this was not good for my future health. Suppose that every time I came upon an intricately useful object, something fashioned out of the thought of man or nature. Suppose that I should begin to deem its usefulness of so much greater importance than my natural hunger to discover the secrets of this usefulness I would in time forget and disregard this innate hunger al-together.

The dire results of this sort of undernourishment have already been told. I escaped them because my father was a worthy Highbelovian. The fact that my contentment with myself was making me, for the moment, a peaceful and untroublesome baby did not concern him. His object was not to see that I give him the least amount of trouble, but to assure a future for me that would give the least trouble to myself. So he set about, that very moment, to awaken me out of my laziness. He approached the crib and brought his hand close to mine, which I was opening and closing with much cocksure-ness. He held his hand quite motionless. At once, it caught my attention. Im-pulsively, I tried to exert my new found will over it, to make it open and close just as I was able to do with mine. But my father's hand remained motionless. The complacent, self-satisfied smile which had spread over my face began to dwindle. The movement of my own hand quickened, and I gave to the act all the angry energy I could summon, as though I expected to see my will wield the same power over my father's hand as it did over my own. Of course, when his hand continued to remain motionless I burst into tears. For I was furious to discover that my precious will could not be made universally effective. Vainly did I grasp with both my fists the giant hand of my father. Vainly did I exert all my strength in an attempt to move the fingers. But he would not allow them to be moved a hair's breadth.

My father did not comfort me in my anguish. On the contrary, he took great delight in watching my fall. He let me scream out my fury at his hand and did not retreat from the blows I struck at it. He kept firm and quiet before me, making me finally realize that there was nothing in the world I could do to move it. My tears dried slowly, and my foolish will was broken. Before long, the hand became an object of calm interest, and out of my broken desire to dominate its movements arose a great and selfless curiosity. I fell to examining the hand and, to my now more gentle and intelligent touch, the fingers bent before me. But the responsive bending of those great fingers no longer signified a victory of my own vainglorious will. My pleasure now was the pleasure of the eternally curious mind seeking to satisfy its curiosities. My father was pleased with me and smiled. I smiled back then, as though to admit that I had been wrong and that he had been right.

As for toys (as they are known in the mortals' land), Highbelovian children seldom show much interest in them. Children whose progress has been normal would show a decided impatience with, for instance, a set of trains. The only attraction would be in setting it up on tracks and watching it go. The Highbelovian child needs more than the passive pleasure of watching something work for him. The need to use his ingenuity while creating makes the idle toys of mortal children irrelevant and uninteresting. Thus, infants are given, for instance, the links of a chain to piece together, rather than a finished chain to inanely jingle about. And boys at an early age are given wood and implements with which to build miniature boats rather than the boats in the finished state. For when a boy starts sailing a boat made by hands other than his own, he imagines himself owner, captain, and lord of creation, while if he had made the boat himself he would be more respectful toward the problems involved in building and captaining a boat and less blown up about himself. The little mortal boy who, while sailing his ready-made boat, hoots like a siren and takes on the general airs of a mighty sea captain would turn away a Highbelovian lad.

This aversion for ready-made toys, now that I recall it, I noticed to be present in very young mortal children. But the parents, instead of encouraging this fine quality, on the contrary, invariably discouraged it. For I have seen mortal children astonish and anger their parents by smashing their little cars, trucks, mechanical men and animals, the moment these things were put into their hands. And I have seen them go for the fragments with a delight they never showed for the toys themselves, as though here was something to which they could give their hands and ingenuity. Whereas before, there was nothing but a silly article to play with. But mortal parents assiduously set about to break their children of all good habits, and before a mortal child is very old he is quite satisfied to accept the passive enjoyment of all the ready-made wonders that are served to him. Before long, he begins to look upon the entire world as ready-made for his pleasure just as he looked upon his ready-made toys. In the end, he becomes the vacuous center of a ready-made universe.

My father always received my childish inquiries with grave respect. Just because my problems seemed small and trivial to him, he did not bind himself in his own maturity so tightly as to be insensate to my own sense of the importance of these trivialities. More often than not, the thoughts that came to my young mind were of the same stuff that preoccupied men who were hundreds of years older. My father, understanding this, consequently would give his sober and respectful attention to my questions. Like all children in Highbelow (as well as in the Land of Mortals), my questions were endless.

I would ask why we walked by putting one leg in front of the other instead of both feet forward at the same time. I would ask why a rock falls down instead of up, or why our noses are on our faces instead of on the back of our heads. I would ask why boats float on water, why birds fly in the skies. I would ask why the sky is blue instead of red, and why men wear trousers and women skirts instead of the other way around. These and countless other questions would I ask of my father. Silly as they may have sounded to him, he never did me the injustice of making light of them. He realized that the natural spirit of inquiry was showing itself, and that the human hunger to know was making itself felt within me. He rightly understood these questions, so foolish on the surface, to have been inspired by profound and subtle thoughts.

Contrasted to this noble parent, I have the example of innumerable mortal fathers whom I have known, who have laughed this very spirit of inquiry right out of their small sons and made so light of their congenital hunger that they have deliberately starved them into an intellectual death.

By the time I reached my tenth year, my universe had become a highly puzzling one, which demanded an inquiry into its nature. I had already delved independently into such subjects as Physics, Astronomy, Biology, Botany and Zoology, Mathematics, Philosophy, Psychology and the Arts. My mortal readers no doubt will be surprised at this and no doubt call me precocious for my age. Yet lest I be misunderstood, I hasten to add that I could not read or write, nor had I ever seen the inside of a book. How then, I am asked, could I have possibly carried on any reasonable inquiry into subjects so advanced (as the mortals say) as these?

Well, for instance, at the age of two years I was given a bouncing ball, not with the purpose of simple amusement, but to awaken my curiosity on the nature of falling objects. By this time, I had already had several encounters with the stupidly tyrannical side of my will, such as I have described, and I had learned how uninspiring was the pleasure of passively using the forces at my command as compared to the intense excitement of getting at them with my mind in order to understand them. Consequently, the first bounce of the ball as I let it drop to the floor puzzled rather than pleased me. My consciousness was awakened to the curious phenomenon of why things fall. From that moment on, everything that was put into my hands I dropped to the floor and from these experiments I came to a vague generalization that there must be something about the ground that draws everything to it, else why didn't other objects rise up again like the ball. And whenever after I bounced the ball, I did so wonderingly. Never did I stop feeling pleasurably curious about the strange object until years later when the meaning of its action was explained to me. Thus, I had begun the study of Physics.

Then there were also my early delvings into Philosophy, when the meaning of the passage of time first confronted me. I remember listening to the tickings of the clock and wondering why each tick came and went so rapidly, and why one of them did not linger in my ear longer than the others. Why, I wondered as I walked along, did one step follow another, and why was I always just leaving off one step and in the act of taking another actually making things called steps? Were there really such things as steps and clock ticks? If so, why were they so evasive, either coming into being or disappearing but never really "being?" Why couldn't I stop these things if they actually were so, stop them and examine them, and live with them and understand them?

You can see by this how, at the age of nine, I had begun to interest myself in Philosophy, even though I could not yet write my own name. I cannot help but recall here a mortal mother whom I once knew on my ill-fated visit to that land. She was inordinately proud of the facility of her nine year-old boy who apparently could write almost any word mentioned. I remember how put out she was with me when I failed to be moved in the least by this. I had to explain that in Highbelow words are considered lastly in the procedure of learning, and that we consider it natural that a child must first have thoughts to write about before he has any need of writing. I told my friend that when the thoughts of a Highbelovian child broaden to the point of wanting to use words upon them, then is writing taught. By that time, so dominant are thoughts over words that learning to write becomes an inner necessity. The result is that he learns quickly and well. But he realizes that he has made stimulating progress in many areas of thought without knowing how to write or spell and so he does not consider this new acquisition as anything but ordinary. As time goes on, he grows into manhood and into the ways of all good Highbelovians, whose indifference to the mortal art of wordery gives them the habit of giving their energies mainly to thinking and incidentally to talking.

But then you see, mortal men, unlike the Highbelovians, have each other's pride to deal with, so the importance of wordy persuasion comes first and the necessity of solitary and wordless thought is only incidental and sometimes utterly lacking. So you see how completely the tables are changed. For if in Highbelow a man were to talk merely to impress his fellows with his superiority, he would shrink badly and become very poor in health, whereas in the mortals' land, the absence of this kind of talk dooms a man to ignominy. Proficiency in it assures him a high position in the community, such as the head of the government or a professorship in a seat of learning. But alas, the contradictions of these two peoples breed out of each other as rapidly as one can think, and if one dwells upon them long, one is sure to become quite dizzy.

I remember how futile were my explanations of Highbelovian education when I was in the Land of Mortals. People everywhere, and especially those in charge of education in the larger cities, were eager to hear the secrets of our "system," as they called it. My natural Highbelovian capacity to think clearly and to keep in mind the relation of one thing to another as I talked overwhelmed my tiny friends who, as you shall see, looked upon me either as a superior being, or as the product of an enlightened method of education. Of course when I explained that there was no system at all, and that we even had no word for it in our language, my listeners either winked at me, as though they appreciated my joke, or else considered me an unmitigated liar. So strong was their faith in their "systems" of this and that, that they would not believe that I had come by (what seemed to them) my advanced intelligence quite naturally. Nowhere would people accept my answers to their questions. In the face of the superior power of my mind and body they clung ever more doggedly to their beliefs, as though they were afraid that I might prove them to be worthless.

And, of course, what with their insidious pride disease, the mortals refused to look into the state of human affairs in Highbelow or to give credence to them, for to do so would be to admit to the possibility of a more serviceable approach to life than their own. For it is the mortal habit, as I observed, to keep their pride intact at all costs. Thus I've noticed that when they talk they do so firstly to defend and justify what they are saying and only secondly and incidentally to say what they have to say. They will go to any lengths to impose their pride of self over the same pride of self exhibited in anyone they are with. And when I came along, quite innocent of any such feelings, and stated in a natural way what was on my mind, why then of course they thought that I was being patriotic about my homeland and that I was giving more than the ordinary measure of blown up pride. In their eyes, I was saying extravagant things and they considered me a liar and a braggart. But if I had been lying or bragging, I would have only been doing in an open way what they were doing shadily and indirectly. But you could not convince them of this and I did not try.

When I told them, for instance, that we had no system of education they refused to believe it, not because they cared whether or not Highbelow had one, but because the absence of such a system would make their own seem superfluous. Such a thought was not to be tolerated. Consequently, without further investigation, they disposed of me in their own minds as a great liar. Yet in the face of my vastly superior intelligence, they could not help but fear me. I was a source of great consternation. Between defending their institutions against my simple words and defending themselves against my power of mind, they involved themselves in the most hopeless confusion. To take me seriously would be to annihilate their tradition of life. Not to take me seriously would be evading the fact of my fearfulness. The consequence was that they laughed at me with their faces and hero-worshipped me in their hearts.

And here I am today, a sick man as a result of that hero worship. For as a true Highbelovian, I was not deceived by their words. I saw into their hearts, and what I saw embedded in me the first germ of all that I have suffered since. For the first time, I saw that I was better than another man. I began *looking down with pride*. And from that moment on, the disease spread within me until it completely took possession. It was then that I began this book.

回回回

The Happy and Unhappy People

Up to this point I have made it seem that all the people in Highbelow measure up to the standards I have set forth. This is far from true. I have not deliberately perverted any of the facts. Yet by stressing one side of Highbelovian society to the exclusion of the other, I have made my homeland appear to the mortal reader like one of his Utopias. This impression has been enough, I am sure, to discredit the existence of such a place as Highbelow and to give the reader as low an opinion of the poor author as he has of himself. But I can, and presently will, show that there are Highbelovians who are far from being as consistently healthy as the prototypes I have set forth in the person of my father and the associates of my youth.

We actually have in Highbelow what amounts to a division of the people into two classes, to use a mortal word. They may be called the Expanders and the Shrinkers, or more generally speaking, the happy-healthy ones, and the unhappy-unhealthy ones. The Expanders produce the good and useful things in life, and the Shrinkers barter these products among themselves. The Expanders build all dwelling houses, paint walls, carve furniture, grow food, and weave garments. In fact, they are responsible for every man-made object in Highbelow. The Shrinkers buy this labor at a universally stable price of so much an hour, then proceed to worry themselves into premature death over the business of bartering the Expanders' wares among themselves.

The Shrinkers, who are usually infected with all four of the *Fatal Maladies*, come up to about the waist of a mature Expander. They form what amounts to a society of their own and stand in awe and fear of the healthy workmen who, unaware, take the commanding position in the community. And I believe that it is this indifference to the power which they have over the Shrinkers which makes the Expanders appear so fearful to their less healthy fellows. It is like the worshipful awe with which mortal men regard their machinery as it performs valuable work without demanding an acknowledgement of gratitude or praise.

Rarely do mortal men encounter this phenomenon in fellow humans. And when they do, they do not recognize the miracle of it until after the rare one is dead. Then they all become conscience stricken and pity the departed for his failure to gain recognition during life. Little do they realize that the pricks of conscience they feel are unwarranted, and that the rare one asked for their praises no more in life than he does in death. Confronted with this fact, they either refuse to believe it, or, when they do, they make a god of him as they did of the man Jesus Christ. And in the same sense, they do this with their machines. They cannot understand how anything can do them a service and not ask to be thanked. Consequently, they have their veneration of charity, of unselfishness, of patriotism, and of all the other virtues they consider godlike.

In some such way do the Shrinkers look upon their superiors, the Expanders. The standard of living among the Expanders being consistently simple, they are quite satisfied with the eternal so-much-an-hour that they get for their labor. However, it must be constantly borne in mind that the Expanders are always in an almost perfect state of health, and consequently have no ambitions beyond the will to produce. The Shrinkers, on the other hand, engage in a sort of warfare among themselves, which results from the ravages of *looking down with pride*. Of all the *Four Maladies*, this one attaches itself most viciously. It is indeed the most pernicious of all. For once a man becomes infected with it, the very nature of it forces the victim to actually take part in his own downfall. The Shrinker begins with *looking down* upon his fellow Shrinkers. Once he has a taste of the satisfaction of *looking down with pride*, he is driven by the desire to increase the illusion and double his satisfaction. So he joins in the war of personal prides which the Shrinkers wage among themselves.

The means he uses to superimpose his pride over the other Shrinkers, who are likewise engaged, are so absurd as to be unbelievable. For instance, he will buy a commodity made by the hand of an Expander, who in his healthy state never suspects that the Shrinker buys it for any other but its intended use, and proceed to market it among the other Shrinkers at the highest price he can attain. Of course, he has no difficulty in getting a price that is far above what he paid because his buyers take pride not so much in the quality of the commodity itself, but in the price that they are able to pay. Thus, their possessions come to mean nothing. The only satisfaction they get proceeds from their pride in the purchase price. They are fond of showing off their possessions to everyone. And in order for the true value of each article to be understood at a mere glance, everything, from serving dishes to houses and lots, is marked with tags which plainly state the prices paid. A visitor to a Shrinker's home will be led about the house and made to scrutinize the price tags of every article in it. The owner, during these exhibitions, takes the greatest satisfaction in his prices. He will call special attention to those tags that show the most absurdly high figures, and he will expect his guests to look crestfallen at the sight of a really rare price. The guest, on his part, will be secretly comparing his own price tags with those of his host, and if he finds that his host has over-bought him, his evening will be ruined. On the other hand, the host, upon noticing the falling spirits of his guest, will consider the evening a great success.

I know of one case where the two holders of the highest price tags in Highbelow got together. They were two of the smallest men at large and deadly enemies. The one who was called Slother was cordially invited for dinner by the other known as Billfolder. Only the select sickest few were invited to be present, and the whole community of Shrinkers was agog with excitement for weeks prior to the event. Which would impose his sense of importance over the other? Which would it be, Slother or Billfolder?

On the evening of the occasion, the Elite of Shrinkerdom assembled at Billfolder's house. It was an enormous building with the ceiling high enough to comfortably house the tallest Expander in Highbelow. But this spaciousness, or what seemed to the stricken little assemblage as such, was nothing but ordinary ampleness of space to the workers who had built the place. Across the front of the building was a large plaque upon which was painted the price paid by the owner, somewhat like the mortals' house numbers, though much greater in size and much more conspicuous. Assembled inside, the guests wandered around observing with great admiration and secret envy the enormity of the figures which every chair and table, every carpet and curtain displayed. Slother was late and the last one to arrive, making sure that his host would not suspect the anxiety with which he had been *looking forward* to the evening.

Billfolder received him cordially after the manner of a man who was being kind to an unfortunate inferior. Dinner was served and the food and service, though no different from the usual fine and simple productions of Expander workmen, bore the highest price tags the guests had ever seen. In the face of such munificence the spirits of the party, from the start, began to fall, and the host, observing the disquieting effect of his price tags, became gayer and gayer. But as time went on, and one tag outdid the next, Slother, unlike the rest, remained imperturbable. Everyone kept eyeing him, noticing with wonder and admiration how confident he appeared. Billfolder, on the other hand, was not worried, for he had even more wondrous prices to display after dinner.

After the meal, (which had been served by Shrinkers tiny beyond all recall) the guests retired to the reception room and immediately the exhibition began. Billfolder led everyone from one room to the next, or rather he led Slother and everyone else followed. As time went on and one tag after another failed to manifestly impress Slother, Billfolder began to lose his perfect self-possession. The guests marveled more and more, not so much at the rare price tags that Billfolder displayed, but at the assurance in Slother's manner that he could show better prices than anything Billfolder possessed. Billfolder's poise gradually wore down. One thing after another failed to impress his guest, until finally he brought the company into his bedroom and showed the price tag attached to his own plain bed in the manner of a drowning man grasping at a last straw. The price seemed fabulous to everyone present and a murmur of admiration passed through the room. Billfolder watched Slother desperately, hoping to see a hint of defeat in his face. But it was plain that the victory was Slother's, for he remained unworried. On the contrary, he could not contain his jubilation any longer and letting out a whoop he grabbed the beaten Billfolder by the arm and dragged the poor man out of the house, followed closely by the gathering.

In this way, he marched his vanquished host to his own home not far down the street. There he completed the slaughter by displaying tags that doubled the amounts in which Billfolder had taken such pride. The poor man in a panic of devastating humiliation shrank to the size of a serving maid, and from that moment was exiled from polite society. He became a butler in the service of one of the taller, less important Shrinkers, and though he served well and submissively, he lingered only a short time and was finally consumed by *looking back* with regret. One morning he failed to appear with the master's breakfast. In the pantry they found his clothes in a heap and everyone realized that poor Billfolder had finally worried himself into oblivion.

Though the victory in this case went to Slother, he paid dearly for it. He survived Billfolder by only a year or so. His success in putting Billfolder to shame blew up his pride to such a point that he continually felt as though he were going to burst. In reality, he shrank so fearfully in size and spirit that his increased opinion of himself was more than he was able to take care of.

The belief that he was a supremely important person was so out of proportion to his actual insignificance that it bloated him. But the bloating was all imaginary. What was real was the fact of his shrinkage. Though slower than that which resulted from Billfolder's malady of *looking up with humility*, his of *looking down with pride* was no less fatal. There was no check to Billfolder's malady, for he became so completely conscious of his ignominy that nothing could bring him back. Slother, on the other hand, being a man of property, kept on buying from the Expanders, and although the humility which he felt in their austere presence served as a check to his pride, it did not last long. One morning not long after Billfolder had shrunk away, Slother's servant found his bed empty, save for the telling presence of the departed's night clothes.

I have mentioned this incident only to show how glaring is the contrast between the two classes of Highbelovians, contrasts, as the mortal reader will notice, that are as fully marked as anything that exists between the classes into which mortals divide themselves. There is one main difference, however, apart from the smaller ways in which Highbelovian and mortal classes differ, and that is the persistency with which one class ignores the other in Highbelow. The very essence of the Expanders' perfect health lies in their complete unawareness of the common ambition—of trying to outdo each other—that dominates the Shrinker's community.

Lacking entirely the competitive spirit, an Expander would be incapable of deriving the slightest satisfaction from destroying a fellow being, such as Slother found in the destruction of his competitor in pride, Billfolder. For you see, to an Expander work is real and rewards are unreal, save for the simple necessity of getting a reasonable and steady return on his labor. To a Shrinker the reverse is true. For he believes that reward is the reality of work and that work itself is a disagreeable interlude that precedes its main function. As a consequence you find him, when he works at all, doing so by sheer force of will as he gets it over with as quickly as possible so that he may sit back and look with pride upon what he has done.

Due to his loathing of work, the Shrinker finds the doing of it far more arduous than it really is, and as a result he is deluded with the idea that he is an exceptionally hard working man. The fact of the matter is that he is profoundly lazy. And of course he cannot but wonder at the ordinary productiveness of an Expander, which to the Shrinker seems inhumanely colossal. It never occurs to him that the Expander lives in his work, that he is so entirely bound up in the work that the fruits of it stand in no relation to the force that produced them. With his mind given completely to the function of work, the Expander uses all the time that the Shrinker spends in being vain about what he is doing, and as a consequence he produces on a scale that makes the Shrinker feel knee-high to him. And feeling knee-high in Highbelow is enough to make one knee-high. This simple fact is the crux of the dilemma.

After all, the mania for price tags among the Shrinkers is a direct outcome of their being so woefully conscious of their disadvantage. In dealing with Expanders they, one and all, try to appear as though they *look down upon* them. It is indeed absurd to see a little Shrinker receiving the wares of a towering Expander trying with all his might to patronize the giant. Being as susceptible as he is to all sorts of delusions, his very manner will temporarily dispel his fear of his superior and make him believe that he is actually what he is making himself appear to be. But then, when later he considers the true state of affairs, he becomes so panic-stricken over the humility of his position that he proceeds at once to redeem his lost pride at the expense of his more vulnerable fellow Shrinkers.

The price tag idea seems to have been the only possible way out. It was conceived out of an extreme urgency. The Shrinker, confronted with the prospect of being annihilated by his overwhelming sense of fear and inferiority, naturally selected the only means he had to check the disease. Being so anxious about himself, he had neither mind nor inclination for honest work, which was the only alternative. As a result, he invented the price tag. It was the child of his great necessity. It brought him pride where pride was sorely needed. It gave him a new lease on life. And yet, though it served to prolong his days, it really only substituted a lingering death for a quick and merciful one. If he had not thought of the price tag, there would never have been Shrinkers in Highbelow. Upon emerging from the immunity of youth, the man who was too sorely stricken with *looking up with humility* would have had nothing to counteract his humility had it not been for the price tag. At this critical life stage, almost every man is stricken more or less with *looking up with humility*, for it is the first time in his twenty-five years that he becomes relatively aware of himself.

He has the choice of two alternatives, namely of either rising above his indisposition and freeing himself of himself through useful and gratifying work, or of bolstering himself up with an anxious ambition to acquire a fortune in price tags that would give him the security of lordliness that he was inclined to believe would cure him. If there were no such thing as price tags, the weak would disappear before they had the chance to do any harm. For

35

there would not be a single straw to cling to. As it is, they are welcomed into the Shrinker's society where they are offered every available means of gaining a pride large enough to offset the humility that runs rampant among the people there.

The newcomer always towers above the older members of the society and as a consequence is patronized by everyone. He comes to them absolutely tagless, but they give him credit for an ambition to become tag wealthy and to some day rate high in the community. A young newcomer is closely watched for any signs of ability. If he shows any gift at all for swindling and clever unscrupulous trading, he is looked upon as promising. And as he becomes more and more successful, and smaller and smaller in height, his position in the community becomes securer. He may even shrink to the power of a Slother. The trick here, however, is not to have more pride than humility, but to keep a good balance between the two. But if the young man is enterprising and energetic, he will be doing a great deal of humiliating dealing with the Expanders and just as much trading in pride with his fellow Shrinkers. In this way he can become ever so small and important without actually shrinking away. It is only when a Shrinker gets an overdose of humility, such as Billfolder got, or when he becomes swamped in pride, like Slother, that he is swiftly killed off. Barring such accidents as these, a Shrinker can linger on for thirty or forty years. But the newcomer to Shrinkerdom does not worry so much about this. He is far too busy swindling his way up from the bottom.

Activity in Shrinkerdom, then, amounts to a means for the people to take their minds off their *Maladies*. Since the sole motivating force of their lives arises out of the *Maladies*, it is obviously urgent that everyone not only must refuse to admit their existence, but further they must invent another motivating force which would not, as the *Maladies* do, reduce their lives to a hopeless absurdity. They must invent something, then, that would seem to ennoble them. Thus, in order to get away from the devastating fact that the only motifs upon which they are capable of acting are *looking forward with anxiety*, *looking back with longing*, *looking up with humility*, and *looking down with pride*, they invented other sordid activities. The best example, because of its universality, is the business of trading price tags. As I've pointed out, it is the buttress that supports the whole feeble structure. It is the knot that keeps the society from unraveling. In the price tag, the Shrinker perceives the guardian of his own precarious destiny. He knows that he stands or falls by it.

Now of course it would be impossible for him to consider the true reasons for his pursuit of the price tag, such as I have already laid down. The pursuit, in reality, is a getting away from these reasons. It is as though a man who had committed murder should run down the street from the scene of his crime chasing a cat, relieving his conscience by letting himself believe that it is the cat he is chasing, instead of detection of murder from which he is running.

But the Shrinker does not stop at simply chasing the cat. He as much as tells himself that out of the goodness of his heart he is trying to catch it in order to give it food. You cannot blame him for running away from his *maladies*. This is a matter of self-preservation. It is understandable that he should try to forget his innate sickness in the pursuit of a price tag. But to carry on the chase in the name of service, self-reliance, fortitude, hard work, high ambition, and such fine virtues is difficult, I imagine, even for a mortal to swallow.

Other reasons are given that may be more or less true, though out of the mouth of a Shrinker they are lies as big as the imagined virtues. For when a Shrinker compliments a fellow on his shrewdness to beat out the other fellow, he imagines that these qualities too are virtues and thus distorts the truth into complete misinterpretation on all sides.

Some readers may perhaps see a strong resemblance between the shrinking side of Highbelovian society and mortal men in general. Discussion of this is reserved for a place later on. Suffice it to say for the present, that one of the main differences arises from the fact that the Highbelovian Shrinker must accept the standards of the Expander workmen and has no say in the matter, while in the mortal's land the reverse is true. Here, the workers must forgo the right of selecting the standards for their own work, and instead supply the demand of the non-workers. You have there the perverse situation of men weaving rugs into patterns dictated by men who have never had a loom in their hands. Not so in Highbelow. There, there are weavers of rugs, cabinet-makers, and silversmiths as in the Land of Mortals, but they are conceded not only the ability to make the rugs, tables and platters, but also the right to conceive the form that they shall take.

To the mortal reader, it will seem incredible that the product of the workman is everywhere, both among the Shrinkers and Expanders, looked upon as essentially the workman's property no matter through how many different hands it passes. And this brings us finally down to perhaps the basic difference between the people of Highbelow and mortal men. I have never been able to straighten in my mind the queer idea of possession as the mortals conceive it. No doubt the mortal reader will be equally at a loss to grasp the Highbelovian point of view. But I shall present it as best I can and trust to luck that my mortal readers will get some inkling of what to them will seem incredible.

Everyone in Highbelow looks upon articles of daily use as a sort of loan from the men who make them. True, they must pay money for them, but they do so more in the spirit of a rental for the use thereof rather than in the spirit of payment for final possession. In this sense neither the houses in which they live nor the plates from which they eat are looked upon as property of the people who use them. The hand and mind of the man who builds houses are ever present with the people who use them. It is not in the nature of a Highbelovian to take possession of something he has never really possessed. And by possession Highbelovians mean creation. When a man takes a stack of lumber and saws it up and joints it together so that it becomes a useful and beautiful chair, why, then that man has possessed. From this rightful owner the chair may be rented, so to speak, to the man who will benefit by its comfort and beauty. It would be a physical impossibility to consider the chair as his. In his eyes nothing belongs to him but the very function of his own work. If he is a weaver of rugs, the patterns, as he makes them form in the loom, belong to him. If he is a farmer, the wheat that springs from the ground, out of the seed that he has buried with his own hands, belongs to him. To him, the act of making something exist where nothing existed before is an act of possession. This and this alone. The fruits of other men's labor are his benefits, not his possessions.

Of course, I am speaking of the Expanders. For they supply the society with every man-made object it uses. They work as they please, at one with their own inevitable destiny which bids them the meaning of their lives upon the earth. To fulfill this destiny is all the satisfaction they need.

It would seem that the scheming Shrinkers could take advantage of the workers. Indeed they would like to, but this is not the case. Consider first that Expanders furnish the Shrinkers with all their worldly equipment. Satisfied to be paid for their labor at a constant wage of so much an hour, the Shrinkers have no incentive that would influence them to work according to the vain requirements of a man suffering from *looking down with pride*. The Expanders have the upper hand and simply turn their products over to those of their fellows, Shrinkers or Expanders, who can use them and who will pay them the standard price. Thus, the Shrinkers' homes are filled with the same fine and simple workmanship as the homes of the Expanders. A mortal could not tell that the inhabitants are of such a different stamp as they really are. The only clue would be in the price tags that adorn the Shrinkers' benefits (or possessions, as they are known to the mortals).

No doubt, if the Shrinkers had the power they would have the workers cover the exteriors of their buildings with the gaudiest gilded ornament that could be conceived and, thus, exploit a life-sustaining craftsmanship to their own prideful ends. But fortunately, they have to rest content with their price tags and confine the noise of their competition to themselves. And it is better thus, for the price that the Shrinker paints across the front of his house, cruel as it may be to the simple beauty of the architecture, is not near what it might be could he come out of his laziness long enough to get to work and express in ornament his anxious desire to be admired.

In the absence of a real variance in the quality of the Expanders' products, it was, of course, necessary for the Shrinkers to invent a way whereby they could make one article appear more valuable than the next. Any man who wanted a large price for, say, a well-made bed, could not announce that it was an exceptionally well-made bed, having a quality that other beds lacked. He could not demand more money for it. He could not appeal to a love of genuine quality in his prospective buyers, for genuine quality was simply expected and taken for granted. The only thing the trader could do was appeal to his fellow Shrinkers' weaknesses. He could set up an establishment and appeal to the worst sufferers from *looking down with pride*. These were the people who were always willing to pay tremendous sums for anything whatsoever, whether or not they needed the articles in question, and whether they could or could not afford to pay the prices asked. These were the people to whom pride in great price tags was the sustaining force of their unhappy lives.

It became the ambition of every Shrinker to work up a clientele of this sort. For if it became known that his prices were huge, and his regular customers correspondingly small, why, then, this man was made. People would consider it something indeed to have dealings with him. The higher his prices became, the higher his reputation would soar until his store would be considered almost holy ground, and he himself quite a dignitary. He would stalk around the place like a king in his palace, and he would look down rather contemptuously upon such people who would dare enter to consider buying.

But such success as this is exceptional. It takes a cunning with which only the most self-concerned are gifted. When one considers it, it must be a most amazing person who can magic people into paying him twenty times what an article is worth. Men such as this are few and far between. Not many can stand the strain. For indeed, it is almost a moral impossibility to keep oneself alive in the face of a self-pride so large as to induce people to pay for the

privilege of dealing with one. The mortality, consequently, among the pro-
prietors of ultra exclusive establishments is extremely high, and at no time
are there more than a few in existence.

Fewer even are the men who have achieved such success and retired. For
though the gesture of retiring is a glorious one, it is, for many reasons, death
dealing. But the dangers involved are obscured by the great gratification
that comes with the homage of a community. People recognize in such a
man a pride so intact that it no longer needs its daily swindle to support it.
The man as much as tells the Shrinking world that he can get along very well
without it. And that, of course, brings the community to its feet. It is everywhere regretted that so exceptional a person is not spared longer. When
people hear of the death of a retired man they shake their heads and wonder
at the perversities of a life which would bring a man to his hard gained goal
only to snatch him away before he has time to enjoy it. They ponder the futility of their lot and wonder why the fruits of their labor, which is the privilege not to labor, are so poisonous. And so the announcement of the death
of a retired man will cause the whole community to shrink perceptibly. For a
moment, one and all fall prey to their anxieties. The future becomes black
with unfulfillment and men ask themselves, "To what end, oh Price Tag?"

I have been speaking of exceptions, however. It is not given to the average
Shrinker to do nearly so well as this by his pride. Only the cleverest can
hide his anxieties behind an indifferent front, can muster up enough self-
control to appear sufficiently independent. Most Shrinkers have not the patience to bide their time, nor the nerve to mark their wares exorbitantly high
and say, "Here you are. Take it or leave it." They are most of the time so
completely the victims of their anxieties that they want to make their fortunes overnight. As a result, among the common run of traders there is the
most vicious competition involving all kinds of schemes whereby each tries
to take away the trade of the other.

The main means employed in the war for the price tag market is known as
overselling. If, for instance, a common bed dealer should buy a lot of them
from Expander craftsmen at the rate of two dollars a bed he will, let us say,
offer them at twenty dollars each. This is considered an average mark-up for
a store without any great reputation, a store that draws customers who are
not wealthy enough and who have not the courage of an extraordinary pride
to deal in more exclusive establishments. The beds, then, are offered at
twenty dollars apiece, with a twenty dollar price tag attached. Now obviously there is no honor in a bed with a mere twenty dollar tag, so the only

purchaser that could be expected would be one who was truly in need of a bed. If the dealer should find that at the moment there was no market for beds, he would have to try his luck with his price tags. He would write out a huge advertisement that might run like this:

SPECIAL OFFER
$100 Tags
A limited supply attached
to beds
$20

In this way the trader brings into his shop the bargain hunters who have not the means to go to the shops that really count and pay face value for high priced tags. They are offered in this way a roundabout means of buying themselves a most convincing illusion of grandeur at a price to suit their limited means. People know, of course, by the anxious and driven looks on their faces that they are of the common run, so they really fool no one but themselves. But so anxious are they to appear to be important in society, so ambitious to at least appear better than their neighbors, that the traders find them ready to swallow their most absurd offers.

But let us suppose that the trader in beds has a competitor around the corner whose trade falls off as a result of the aforesaid advertisement. There is nothing he can do but retaliate in a like manner. He will offer tags of $110 for $20, and his rival will come back with $120 tags. And in this way one will outraise the other until their business comes to a standstill with everyone watching the dealers litter the streets and building walls with advertisements, fighting for every inch of available space to write their offers in the most visible spots. The tags they offer by the end of the day will have become so absurdly large that the poor average Shrinker will be frightened away by the prospect of owning a price tag too magnificent to live comfortably with his low opinion of himself. In this way do our friends the dealers cut off their own noses to spite each other's faces.

Inasmuch as the mania for price tags is the dominating impulse that comes out of Shrinkerdom, it is obvious that the trader can exert a profound influence over everyone. In knowing that a man will do most anything to gain possession of high price tags, he realizes that he can persuade him into any frame of mind, lure him into any extravagance, in fact, make him believe almost anything he tells him.

In their hearts, the Shrinkers know each other well. They know that each and every one of them is mainly concerned with running away from himself. They know that to stand up to themselves and inquire honestly into the state of their own beings would fling them into such an anxious state that death would be immediate. So it is tacitly understood among them all that the last thing in the world they want to hear is the truth about themselves. They live in mortal fear of the possibility that one among them may mention the true state of human affairs in Shrinkerdom. And it does happen, rarely, that one of them goes completely mad under the pressure of the unacknowledged reality within him, and flings out the revealing words that strike such terror into the hearts of all who hear him that he is hustled away to jail where he is kept until he comes to his senses again.

In general, however, they find each other only too willing to forget what they are, and only too eager to help each other in the belief that they are something infinitely better. The possession of the price tag is the main purveyor of this illusion, while the noble service of marketing this life-sustaining commodity is another. . . .

                                                     ❧ November 22, 1929 ❧

PART II

(Wellfleet, Massachusetts — June, 1971)

After much retrospection, I am convinced that the words you have just read were written in another existence. I believe that Anoth and I are one and the same, and that the past sixty-five years of my life on earth have been a kind of purgatorial continuum of my life in Highbelow. Though I have no clear recollection of when or where the writing was done, my sense of identity with the words and phrases, persons and places, and the Highbelovian way of life is so absolute that there can be no doubt that I was indeed the author.

There are other matters concerning the manuscript about which I am not so certain. For one thing, there is the abrupt and unexplained way the writing ends when one would least expect it to. Why the sudden silence, as though the writer had dropped dead in the act of setting about to begin a new paragraph? In probing through the foggy density of a strange and far away memory, I must tell you here and now, incredible as it may seem, I recall that although I did not drop dead in the sense that we on earth know it, I did suddenly simply cease to exist. Indeed, the more I dwell on it, in fact, the more clearly I relive the sensation of falling down and away, following what seems to have been an uncontrollable spasm of anxiety and frustration which had plagued me in my efforts to get on with my story. My next awareness is of arriving head first in the present world, marking the beginning of a bewildering new existence which has had a persistent proclivity to deny its own reality by always mistaking itself for either its own dead past or projected future.

The process of being born into this world, as some of us know through vague memory and others through psychiatric research, is a painful and unwanted experience and is violently resisted by the victims as is indicated by the baleful howling that ensues. Some, it has been found, never reconcile themselves to this forced entry into the world outside the womb and remain forever alien to life on earth, as they long to return to the benign security of their prenatal existence.

In my own case, my life has been permeated with an undefined longing for an unremembered, but strangely magnetic, previous existence. If one wishes to explain this as the common human impulse to return to the womb, I shall not argue that point. Yet, in the light of the vision I have of existence as it is lived in that other world called Highbelow, I am strongly inclined to give credence to the probability that I lived through a previous life as a member of the Highbelovian race and that ever since my appearance on earth, I have longed to return to it. In this way, my earthly life has been an anxious, wishful, looking forward to the revival of a past existence, which, as can be readily seen, is a cruelly anomalous and self-defeating condition. For to be looking forward and back simultaneously is even worse than that of any of the Highbelovian afflictions about which you have read. For at least the Highbelovians suffered their *Maladies* one by one and not doubled and redoubled into monstrously inflated syndromes such as I have suffered here on earth.

The shock of being born helpless into an alien world is, as we all know, cushioned and comforted by the protective maternal presence. The warmth of the mother's body, the loving engulfment of her soft arms and gentle hands that every infant experiences, act as a consoling replacement of prenatal comforts and contentments. The child is as tenderly weaned from life in the womb as, some months later, a considerate mother will gently wean him from her breast. In short, the child, from the minute he is born, for at least the period of his early childhood, is shielded from the necessity to cope with the realities of a new life.

I had the misfortune of being denied the protection of this benign maternal concern after only ten months of life on earth. For my mother, whom I remember as a high-spirited and beautiful being, one day disappeared, leaving me horribly alone in a cold and cruel vacuum that abruptly replaced her warm and reassuring presence. Her death, I am certain, at that particular moment, profoundly affected the whole course of my subsequent existence.

For one thing, I never recovered that brief sense of being rightly at home in this mortal world, which my mother's presence had given me. During my childhood, and on through the years, I have wishfully, sometimes even frantically, sought to attach myself and belong to the times and places through which I was passing. Now and then, here and there, I have been able to persuade myself and those about me that a natural kinship existed between us and that their ways were, by nature, my ways. But I have never been able to deceive myself or others for very long before the alien nature of my character became too obvious to conceal.

Until the recent discovery of the *Highbelow* manuscript, I could only explain my alienation as a perverse accident of birth complicated by an unfortunate childhood. But as I read and reread this account of life in that amazing other world, the realization crept into my consciousness that it was there where I really belonged and that all my difficulties here on earth resulted from the hopeless dislocation of a stranger in a foreign land. For I am now quite certain that what have seemed to me to be the perversities of my nature have been, in truth, acceptable Highbelovian qualities and conditions which under earthly circumstances have always been looked upon as unreasonable and unacceptable eccentricities.

This new discovery of a previous existence has, of course, altered the way my life here on earth now appears to me. Much that previously seemed negative and perverse now, from a Highbelovian point of view, appears purposeful and proper. And it seems to me, now that I have recovered some of my Highbelovian perspective, that almost from my first days on earth I have been trying, vainly for the most part, to reattain my lost Highbelovian ways of doing and seeing in a human climate where they are totally unacceptable. In looking back, my first recollections of life as a mortal will bear out what I say.

It seems that from the very beginning of my self-awareness, my thoughts tended to perpetually turn inward in search of self-confirming identities rather than outward toward a natural merging of self with a friendly and anonymous reality. In my motherless isolation and helplessness, reality was a fearsome chasm of formlessness. I hardly dared look out upon the world, and I withdrew into myself. I worried and sometimes exasperated the hired women who, one after the other, failed to replace my mother. My tight-lipped silence and refusal to eat, laugh, or cry, left them helpless. One nurse after another tried, each in her own way, to restore my health without much success. I ate only what food could be forced down my throat. I suffered the medical and curative ministrations of one practitioner after the other, mostly well-meaning women, in resentful and painful silence. Sullenly and unwillingly, I floundered through infancy to babyhood to early childhood and somehow managed to survive.

Though much of my early life is only vaguely remembered, certain facets do remain vivid. Of the many puzzlements that engross the newly born, the question of identity was a constant obsession. Uppermost, was the identity of myself and the various facets of myself that I could see—my hand, a toe, my genitals—but also the things I could not see, but touch, like an ear or my nose. I was also preoccupied with the sounds that issued from my throat, which could be heard, but to my confusion not touched or seen. While these matters no doubt are the common preoccupations of all babies, I am inclined, since my re-discovery of Highbelow, to connect the obsessional character of my self-searching with a deeply buried, instinctive will to achieve reincarnation of my lost Highbelovian identity here on earth. I can explain in no other way my life-long unhappiness with the conventional earthly identities that I have vainly tried to adopt for the purpose of living peacefully with my fellow mortal men. For the Highbelovian "I" is an entirely different reality from the earthly conception of "self," which is not necessarily a true reality, but more often a concocted image comfortably at home in a make-believe world.

But before I reflect further on this phenomenon, I shall resist the temptation, at least for the present, to speculate about the strange affinity between certain negative aspects of Highbelovian life and the conventional aspirations of mortal men. Though the comparison suggests a shared continuum of existence between the two places, I am not ready as yet to rush headlong to the wild conclusion that comes to mind.

And so I return to the joyless unreality of my early existence. My memory is crowded with bits and pieces of the seen and felt, vague impressions of people coming and going, fragments of incidents that somehow will not sink away into the limbo of the forever forgotten. I remember the stooped over gait of a bald-headed grandfather with his cane and the cackling sound he made, which I suppose was laughter. I remember the somewhat removed but imposing presence of my father, which had little effect on me except for one time when he was confined to his bed with a back ailment. I suppose I cling to the memory of this illness because, for once, someone was palpably sharing a misery similar to the many from which I suffered in silence. I remember blistering both my hands by grasping the exposed iron of a red-hot radiator. I remember the pain, the grease, the bandages, and the exasperating discomfort of changing them. I remember my sister, who was two years older than I, lying down on a landing of the stairway in a wild temper tantrum, kicking out her legs and pounding the floor with her feet while screaming out her frustration at having to leave behind a carriage drawn by two fine horses while she was to be put to bed. I suppose the deep impression this incident has left upon me can be explained by the fact that it never occurred to me to complain about my own frustrations, so an angry outburst from another child seemed strange and somewhat unbelievable.

Few things interested me. I remember no toys or favorite objects except one: a talking machine that was set up in front of the living room windows, or parlor, as I believe it was called in those days. This contraption, which arrived the year between my third and fourth birthdays, caused a great stir not only in the house, but also throughout the neighborhood. I remember seeing groups of people gathered on the street below the open windows to listen to the music and voices that screeched out from the contraption which must have been the first of Mr. Edison's gramophones to appear in our part of town. And while the machine was one of the few things in my young life that attracted my interest, I remember being impressed, and a bit revolted (I could not say why) by the ostentatious way the mouth of the great horn was turned out toward the street to attract the attention of passers by. I repeat this impression here because it comes to me as possibly further proof of my Highbelovian origins. For such a sophisticated reaction at so innocent an age is indeed not to be expected from the newly born of mortal men.

My principle interest in the gramophone was in the music it played. With one exception, (which I will name later) I do not remember specific tunes or songs, though there echoes vaguely in my memory thin, high-pitched nasal voices. Whatever the machine produced, I remember being completely absorbed in it, particularly by certain pieces which became my special favorites. But it was not just the sounds that issued from the thing which held my attention. For the first time in my short life, I was absorbed by a sustained and continued objective interest in a particular facet of my surroundings. It was the enormous horn rising from the comparatively tiny playing mechanism which fascinated me the most. I recall its impressive shape starting from a narrow neck at the base and curving gracefully outward in a series of fluted, longitudinal valleys, which ended in a sharply curved lip to form the enormous, gaping mouth of the chasm from which the sounds were ejected.

I suppose my fascination with the talking machine was observed with a certain relief by the adults around me, for my indifference to the normal preoccupations of a small child must have worried them to the point of exasperated despair. I had no use for the usual toys and flatly rejected the companionship of stuffed animals, dolls, and picture books. This mental and spiritual inertia from which I suffered, no doubt, affected my appetite and my health to the point where, as I learned later in life from my father, there was a question whether I would survive for long. Indeed, my father must have seized upon the signs of this miraculous awakening. For before long I was mastering the operation of the machine. The decision to teach me how to work the precious thing and allow me access would seem to indicate the extent of the desperation to find a cure for my fatally debilitating condition.

As I remember, the playing mechanism involved the insertion and removal of small discs about six or seven inches long, perhaps a couple of inches in diameter. The surfaces of these discs were textured with a pattern of tiny, raised metal pimples following a design, no doubt, dictated by the various sound patterns. I loved the sight and touch of all the many discs, which were stored on a bookshelf near the small table that held the gramophone. The discs, I believe, were each stored in their own box, and each carried a label identifying the music, songs, dialogue or whatever was the special nature of the entertainment.

In playing these discs incessantly, one after the other, I came to know in intimate and totally remembered detail, the words and music of each. The collection soon grew to the point where it became difficult to keep them from becoming so mixed up, I was unable to keep track of my favorites. Not having learned to read, I could not understand one letter, much less one word. But in my eagerness to identify and select at will any tune in the collection that came to mind, I somehow devised a way to cope with the situation through the exercise of what appeared to everyone around me to be a miraculous form of magic, bordering on clairvoyance but which was, in truth, the intelligent ingenuity of a child with good visual memory and, what is more to the point, an overwhelming desire to make use of it.

The people around me, to their amazement, soon discovered that I was identifying specific discs for all the world, by a quick glance at the printed labels, as though I could read the words I saw there. I remember this as truly as anything that has ever happened to me. Looking back through the muddled-headedness that comes with sixty-six years of life on earth, this peculiar ability seems as incredible to me now as it then did to my elders, though I recall that I managed it quite effortlessly and was astonished that people made such a fuss about it. When I try to explain the phenomenon to myself and to recall how the feat was accomplished, I seem to remember associating specific configurations of words and letters with specific songs and tunes so that, in a sense, I rebuilt a small segment of the English language into the special semantics of my gramophone world. When I wished to entertain myself with a particular song or tune, I would call to mind the spoken title and then associate it with the remembered visual aspects of the words printed on the labels. I became quite an expert with this sleight-of-eye operation. For it was not long before the entire collection was at my fingertips.

My accomplishment in the beginning was entirely the innocent and unconscious result of a child's first powerful compulsion to confront and overcome the difficulties standing between him and the solution of a problem that deeply affected his well-being. Once this was done, the innocent aspect of my effort was gradually eroded, as is to be expected in our mortal society, by certain insidiously corrupting influences. It started out pleasantly enough with one of the discs my father loved and never tired of listening. My mother had been gifted with a fine soprano voice, and he loved to listen to her sing. Throughout his life he spoke nostalgically of her singing and even went to great lengths later, when my sister's voice matured to what seemed to be an echo of her mother's, to encourage her to train under well-known teachers. It was as though he were trying to bring an auditory image of his wife back to life.

He would listen intently to my sister as she practiced excerpts and arias from well-known operas. There was one piece in particular that he consistantly asked for called *My Rosary*, which apparently had been one of my mother's stand-bys. My sister sang this melancholy song to him time and again, until it became for me as fixed an auditory memory of her as it had been for my father. Still, this was years later, and at the time in question my father turned to our new gramophone for a renewal of his cherished memory. And, of course, his favorite disc was a harsh soprano rendering of *My Rosary*.

The therapeutic aspect of my new involvement was soon forgotten in the general stir caused by my uncanny ability to decipher words without knowing how to read. My father, recovering from his initial stunned incredility, developed a great sense of personal pride in my achievement. I remember time and again being summoned to the parlor to ask Uncle So-and-So or Mrs. Whoever to name some popular song so that I could astonish them by picking it out from among the stored cylinders and playing it. Of course, I couldn't help but be affected by the overbearing praise that always greeted, what had seemed to me, a simple matter, and it was not long before the innocent aspects of my interest became largely the self-displaying efforts of a bright child whose intelligence was rapidly being corrupted by his elders just as it was beginning to flower.

My father obviously took great pleasure in asking me to play his cherished rendering of *My Rosary*, but I was more impressed with his pride in me than in the song itself. In fact, I remember a sense of irritating monotony after repeating it over and over and over again. Moreover, I could not understand his continued fascination with it. And yet, I always eagerly anticipated the inevitable request. Thus, did I begin to acquire the ways and habits of mortalhood which eventually stripped my character of the last vestiges of my Highbelovian inheritance and left me hopelessly susceptible to the inanities of this earthbound society.

Lest this chronicle becomes just another autobiographical account of an unhappy childhood, I must remind myself and the reader of the compulsion that drove me to add this sequel to the Highbelovian manuscript, which, I now realize, was my own handiwork. My interest in exploring my earthly beginnings has nothing to do with what might be a writer's special delight in a literary exercise. Besides, it should be understood that I am by profession a painter, not a writer, and I would not be here involved was it not for a sense of manifest necessity to find the missing links in the broken continuum of my two lives.

There are questions which I must ask, some of which perhaps can never be answered. For instance, how can the presence of the Highbelovian manuscript in my storage trunk be explained? And though I'm certain that the writing is my own, when and where was it written? Might there have been an interval within my earthly life when I returned to Highbelow? How else can Anoth's reference to his visit to the Land of Mortals be explained? And what about my sense of familiarity with the Highbelovian people and their ways? Did I (or he), as Anoth predicted, succumb to the fatal effects of the Highbelovian *Maladies* and disappear only to be reborn on the 27th of July, in the year 1905, in the city of Chicago to a life that may eventually prove to be the purgatory of a fallen Highbelovian? I expect that the proof of this supposition may be found in my life-long struggle to escape from the tangle of mortal perversities and to reach back to a Highbelovian kind of health and happiness which, though seemingly within my grasp, has always remained cruelly unobtainable.

The reader has seen how, as an infant, exposed as I was to the onslaughts of mortal society after the death of my mother, I withdrew into what was left of my Highbelovian self in a state of silent revulsion. My Highbelovian innocence and intelligence was finally invaded and corroded by the habits and ways of what, for want of a better name, I must call common mortality. For the people who surrounded me were typical mortals who accepted their world as they found it, and who resented the presence of people who did not. My refusal as a baby to respond with smiling compliance to their world must have made me seem like an eccentric and even slightly demented stranger. And I suppose that when I began to respond with signs of a more normally self-concerned egotism, they found me more to their liking. However, as you shall see, there had to be a more radical change in my life than the introduction of a mere talking machine before my rebellious Highbelovian spirit was brought more nearly into conformity with what was expected of me.

Somewhere within my fourth year, Miss May Bowman entered my life. Up until this time women of one sort or another came and went, leaving little impression and remaining, to this day, nameless and faceless. Not Miss Bowman. To a small child she was an inescapably large and powerful presence. She was, in retrospect, a fat, dumpy woman with small, cruel eyes and a harsh voice. There was nothing anonymous about her, and I was made to know from the beginning that I was overwhelmingly in her care.

In speaking of this woman who was to dominate my life for the next nine years, it should be kept in mind that there is no longer any doubt in my mind of my Highbelovian origins, nor that Miss Bowman's new charge was indeed the reincarnation of poor Anoth here on earth. My fate, as deplorable as it would be for an ordinary mortal child, was, as you shall see, an unbearable disaster for a Highbelovian, even a fallen one. Miss Bowman was a woman of almost total ignorance, except for her specialty in which she claimed unquestioned expertise which was restoring vigorous health to children of weak and ailing constitutions. My father had engaged her ostensibly to oversee the upbringing of both his children with the title of governess. Yet, I am sure that he decided upon her principally because of her claim to be talented as a superior practical nurse. In light of his despair over my seemingly incurable disabilities, he no doubt eagerly accepted the woman's boast that within a short time, she would transform my wan and sickly appearance into the picture of vigorous good health.

Little did I know what was in store for me. I do not recall the beginnings of her regime, though she must have first appeared as simply another female presence following the disappearance of her predecessor. I am only aware that one day she was there in all her overbearing and brutal authority. From the first, Miss Bowman set her small, stubborn mind so blindly and fanatically on my recovery that it became a matter of indifference to her what happened to me in the process. It now seems a pity that she arrived before the healing effects of my happy interest in the talking machine could take root. For the precious contraption dropped from sight as the image of Miss Bowman made its appearance. In later years, she often boasted that I would have died without the benefit of her expert care, but today I am certain that she merely compounded my physical difficulties with a brand of spiritual torture that, taken together, required all of whatever was left of my High-belovian powers to survive under her care.

Miss Bowman's principle skills regarding the care of delicate children were actually limited to two: force-feeding and corporal punishment. She made it clear from the start that her authority was absolute. I suspect that she persuaded my father to give her free hand in all matters affecting the welfare of his children. No doubt, she demanded exclusive control over us, and freedom from all interference in carrying out her duties as she saw them. My poor father must have gladly acquiesced to her requirements, happy to be relieved of the kind but ineffectual efforts of the many housekeepers, friends and female relatives who had tried to maintain his motherless household. For with the coming of Miss Bowman, the presence of other people, the sound of laughter and noisy voices around the house disappeared. All at once, I was hopelessly alone with her—her and her tight-lipped determination to break my will and have her way. Even my father seemed to become withdrawn and remote. In looking back, I lose the sense of his intimate presence and see him as a desperately welcome visitor.

Miss Bowman's insistence that I eat every morsel of food she placed before me was at first resisted with silent, lock-jawed determination. However, my father's increasing absences left her free to deal with me in her own special way. For the first time in my life, I felt the pain and humiliation of being slapped in the face with the flat of the hand or rapped on the knuckles with the back of a spoon. Instead of sitting at the table, as befits a boy of four, I was locked back into my baby high chair while Miss Bowman forced spoonful after spoonful of food into my mouth. And when my stomach would retch and rebel and I would throw up what she had labored so persistently to get down, she would shake me roughly, bring in more of her hateful food, and begin the torturous process all over again. Somehow she reasoned that vomiting was my way of fighting her, and force-feeding was to her the winning of a battle against a stubborn adversary. Somehow I managed to survive her feeding ordeal, but the ingestion of food under the aegis of Miss Bowman always remained an altogether revolting task.

It was not long before the shock of these frightening confrontations was replaced by a sense of inescapable enslavement. The woman, it seemed to me, was there, had always been there, and unlike the others would never disappear. At four, my infant memories no longer reached back to touch the lost presence of my mother. My father, save for occasional appearances, was absorbed by the world beyond the house. My six year-old sister suffered her own fate in her own way. And though we, no doubt, found in each other the small consolation of a shared agony, were each alone, each withdrawn into the protective opacity of a child's self-made isolation.

My outer life, in its every waking moment, was exposed to a relentless scrutiny from which the only escape was inward to a private world of make believe where the creature, try as she might, could never follow. And it was from this hiding place, this impregnable refuge from the cruel realities of the mortal world, that I began the long and still continuing struggle to regain my Highbelovian spirit and to somehow find my way back to Highbelow.

My escape into a make-believe reality was sometimes aided by Miss Bowman herself. The brittle dryness of her cruel, insensitive nature found nourishment in an occasional indulgence of a perverse kind of sentimentality and romanticism. Her favorite song, which she tried now and then to render grimly (harshly off key) was a banal love song, whose opening line still echoes horribly in my ears. "Oh believe me," it went, "of all those endearing young charms that I gaze on so fondly today . . ." The words, recalled exactly as I first heard them, continue to revolt me in my old age.

These seemingly soft tendencies in an otherwise brutally hard personality did not fool me, for I knew them for what they were, short interludes of false peace and pleasantness that would appear unexpectedly and then abruptly vanish. However, I learned to make the most of these respites, especially when they involved Miss Bowman's weakness for the new theater of the moving picture. She could not resist the romantic appeal of adventures of savage indians and kidnapped maidens. There was a small theater not far from where we lived. Now and then Miss Bowman, unable to resist the temptation, would take herself to the nickelodeon, as the place was called. But in indulging herself, she had perforce to indulge her two charges, for she did not dare leave them alone. For my part, I became deeply addicted to the picture stories and found in them, not the Highbelovian refuge that I instinctively sought, but an acceptable substitute in a world of cowboys and Indians.

The neighborhood theater was a long, low-ceilinged affair with rows of seats on either side of a downward sloping aisle. I vividly recall the impression upon entering the misty darkness through which a cloudlike stream of light hovered overhead, extending the length of the room until it reached the flickering images that moved about on a wall far in front. Above the entranceway, the buzzing hum of the unwinding reel mingled with the metallic sounds of a pounding piano issuing from a pit at the end of the long aisle. Miss Bowman would lead the way and we would follow, stepping gingerly through the haze looking left and right in search of empty seats. The stream of light above our heads seemed almost within my reach, but I never dared try to touch it, having heard the angry shouts that greeted the taller patrons who walked straight through it without bothering to stoop.

While the theater itself remains clearly discernible, I cannot recall any particular story or picture, though I know that whatever was projected onto the screen greatly excited me; it became the treasure of my imagination and a driving force in my secret life. Curiously, I carried away as vivid an impression of the music as of the picture stories, for the piano poundings not only replaced the missing sounds of voices, gunshots, and galloping horses, but also became the symbolic essence of the images that filled my eyes.

There were two particular musical prototypes which I will never forget and which I can still hear if I listen intently enough. As a young man years later, vague memories were often aroused by certain piano passages of Chopin where the music would sweep up and down the keyboard in a frenzy of almost acrobatic action and excitement. Somehow it always left me with a strange sense of deja-entendu. I was particularly puzzled by a recording that I bought and played on a little portable phonograph when I was living in London at the age of twenty-one. It was a Chopin piano concerto and I wondered why the last movement seemed so extraordinarily familiar. One evening, it dawned on me that the piano player of my childhood had aptly united the melodramatics of Chopin's arpeggios with the breath-taking moving pictures of the nickelodeon's old wild west.

There was another deeply ingrained musical impression that became an essential ingredient of the make believe imagery I invented to escape from reality. Miss Bowman, who obviously found children as boring as they were hateful to her, did everything she could to get me out of her sight as much as possible. I was required to lie down on my bed every day for a long nap, although I only pretended to sleep. I was also put to bed as early as possible and, when my father was away (which was more often than not) I was not allowed to get up until called. During the day I would be let out, like a dog, to "play" in the backyard, which was a large barren area surrounded by a high fence and the back of the house where Miss Bowman would periodically peer through a window to observe me. There was nothing of a constructive nature that I could do. I was given no toys, told nothing, nor taught nothing. I had to invent ways of passing the time and somehow or other, with an assisted by my piano player and the wild west, I did.

Instead of the Highbelovian that I unconsciously longed to be, I became a cowboy. Long stick in hand, which I must have found lying about the yard somewhere, it miraculously became a prancing horse with me in the saddle, streaking in pursuit of a band of savage Indians. There was no beginning and no end to this drama. Suddenly, I found myself on a bouncing horse in the midst of a frantic chase. And so, I would hop and skip with the stick between my legs in an endless circle around the yard. But the magic ingredient of this transformation of a forlorn little boy into a hero on a horse was in the fragment of a song that I would sing. The entire illusion depended on this inane ditty, and I would sing it at the top of my voice over and over again as I galloped over the hills, breathlessly trying to keep the tune and the words in the backyard in the limbo of forgotten things.

> PONY BOY, PONY BOY WON'T YOU BE MY TONY BOY
> DEE-DA-DO, OFF WE GO FAR ACROSS THE PRAIRE
> CARRY ME, MARRY ME, RIDE AWAY WITH YOU
> GIDIAP, GIDIAP, GIDIAP, WHOA! MY TONY BOY.✶

The song went on endlessly, as did the hopping and skipping with a stick between my legs, until the shrill voice of Miss Bowman would wake me from my dream with the hated command: "Come here and eat your apple!"

✶It seems that this song was one of the popular favorites of the day, and was heard wherever music was played—at the pictures and on discs, and on the lips of people everywhere. No one taught me this song. I found it somewhere, somehow, and it has haunted me ever since.

My apple! Of all the hatefully recurring foods she considered indispensable to my survival, my daily apple was the one that, in retrospect, seems to have been the most hateful. More so, perhaps, than even the horrible vegetable soup which simmered interminably on the kitchen stove, giving off a penetrating odor very much like the acrid smell of perspiration. The ritual of *my apple* occurred punctually every day at four o' clock. I had to come running from wherever I was, take the apple from her outstretched hand, and begin the process of ingesting it in her presence. If, in my distaste, I would cautiously nibble at it, I would be forced to attack it more boldly and stuff my mouth with larger bites. The ritual would end when Miss Bowman was satisfied that the thing was eaten "down to the core." Many unsatisfactory inspections took place, and many seeds and shell-like pieces were chokingly spat out before I was dismissed, usually in tears.

My difficulties with the intake of food began, of course, in my infancy and I have already mentioned how, until the arrival of Miss Bowman, I ate only what I chose to accept, which according to everyone was hardly enough to keep me alive. Miss Bowman's idea of remedying this situation was to stuff me with more food than I could keep down. There were certain foods that she considered dietetically essential, which I suspect in certain instances were inspired by the grim pleasure she took in torturing me with my special aversion to them. The proof of this tendency toward a kind of gastrophrenic sadism was in the way she would challenge me with a bowl of applesauce, which curiously happened to be one of the few things she made that I found edible. Grateful for a respite of this kind, I would indicate that I liked it, which she calculated was a sly attempt to fool her, at which point a nasty smile would cross her fat face. She would tell me there was no need to pretend, because she knew very well that I really hated the stuff. Was it not made of my special enemy, the apple? The manifest pleasure she took in the discomfort she was certain I was concealing, gave me the rare satisfaction of a few fleeting moments of secret triumph.

Over the years, my four o'clock apple became the personification of my fear and hatred of the woman and the mark of the misery which she inflicted. I came to dread the approach of the hour of four. There was never a day in all the dreary nine years of her regime, no matter what the circumstance, when the ritual was dispensed with. I remember one day when I was perhaps eight or nine years-old and was walking home from school with my sister, in gloomy anticipation of the apple that awaited me. I remember, as the distance lessened between me and the pending ordeal, the prospect of facing up to the woman and her iron will became suddenly intolerable. The thought seized me like the grasp of a giant arm that I must stop walking toward the apple, turn around and run hard in the opposite direction. And without further thought, that is exactly what I did, leaving my sister staring after me in amazement.

I ran frantically for several blocks, but soon slowed to a walk. A strange calm overtook me as I lost sight of everything but the miracle of sudden freedom. As I continued on, Miss Bowman became unreal and ceased to exist. With no plan in mind, I stopped in front of a cigar store where a man was posting the latest baseball scores. I sat on a trash box facing the window and lost myself in the letters and numbers that covered the store window. How long I sat there I cannot say, but I remember looking down the street and to my horror catching sight of Miss Bowman striding grimly toward me followed by a crowd of boys whom she, no doubt, had sent out to find me. What I am getting to here is what happened when she got me home.

The apple ritual took place on schedule with more choking and retching than usual, for I was sick with anticipation of the beating that I knew Miss Bowman was gradually leading up to.

Though the woman constantly indulged her passion for corporal punishment, she usually confined herself to sharp slaps in the face or stinging blows on the hands (palms outstretched) or on the buttocks with a dressmaker's ruler or hair brush or, lacking a weapon, with her large fat hand. But there were special occasions like the present one where her wrath would match the passion of her sadistic compulsions, and it was during these times wherein she outdid herself. After the apple was examined and the core disposed of, I was shoved, numbed with fear, into my room and commanded to take off my clothes and lie down on the bed. Dumbly, I did what I was told and curled up with my arms around my head and my back exposed to her. And then the blows began, slowly at first, and then harder and faster. I remember the swish of the whip-like stick she used, and then the loud smacking sound as it struck my skin forcing me to scream with pain and despair. And as the pace and power of the beating increased, I finally wriggled about the bed in a vain attempt to avoid the blows. There came the moment when her frenzy must have reached the point where whatever caution she had used in aiming her blows was gone. It was then when the stick struck me on the penis and I screeched with pain. Suddenly the blows stopped and she quickly examined me, and I noticed through my tears that sudden concern had replaced the tight smile of crazy anger which was always fixed upon her face on these occasions. As it happened, I was not badly hurt, but the accident apparently had frightened her and I was told to dress. The relief I felt was purely physical, for there was no release from the fearful certainty that the present respite was only temporary and soon there would be another day like this one.

I have often wondered how my father, who was an intelligent man of the world, could have failed to learn the true nature of the woman he had so totally entrusted with the care of his two children. Though he never remarried, I believe it was at this time, some three years after my mother's death, that he roused himself to rejoin friends and associates in the world outside his home to begin a new life. To do this, unquestioning faith in Miss Bowman was doubtlessly necessary to his peace of mind. His high opinion of her was probably as wishful as it was sincere. She must have sensed this, because she always managed to be a paragon of good will and proper behavior whenever he was present. I used to observe with a mixture of revulsion and relief her transformation that took place at the sound of a latchkey at the front door, a sound which never thereafter has failed to lift my spirits wherever I might be.

There was a certain animal cunning in the tactics she used to cover up any evidence of the cruelties which she inflicted on us. When she first arrived, there must have been another servant in the house with her because years later, in revealing the whole ugly story to one of my aunts, I was astounded to hear her confess that an amiable black woman who helped out in the kitchen, upon quitting the job, complained to her that she could not bear the way the governess treated the children. My aunt had done nothing about it because she couldn't believe the woman was telling the truth. But never again, through all the dreary years of her reign, did Miss Bowman allow anyone to invade her domain that might challenge her authority or spy on her. Apparently, she encouraged my father in his long absences by her scrupulous behavior in his presence.

What now seems so incredible is the way she imposed silence on my sister and me by freezing us with the fear of the horrible, unspoken revenge which we were certain she would take if ever we told on her. For nine long years, her two young victims were actually used as witnesses to the virtues she claimed and then discarded as soon as no one was present. There were no words exchanged between the tyrant and her subjects on the matter of tattling tales. Miss Bowman did not need words. She had a way of slightly compressing her lips and blankly staring at us in a way that would stop our hearts. And she managed the signal so only we would notice. This was always followed by a kindly smile which stung like a slap in the face.

By the time a year had passed, Miss Bowman had become a permanent fixture. Her overbearing presence dominated my waking hours. There was no single detail of my daily existence that she did not dictate. Throughout the long days, I was driven by the force of her powerful will and her brutal methods of exerting it. Still, my enslavement was not total, for hidden deep within my hopelessness was a secret will that would not bow to her, an inner strength that would sustain me in the trying years ahead. Like every mortal child, I had to find my way through the cruel stupidities of the adult world in the struggle to recapture that state of grace that had been mine to begin with.

I now firmly believe that all mortals are born, as was I, with the perfect outlook of a healthy Highbelovian and that somewhere along the line of life that leads finally to the grave, we lose the last link with the genius of our infancy and early childhood and finally become totally degraded into unregenerate mortalhood. Thus the lost, corrupted soul of May Bowman confronted and challenged the fallen Highbelovian known as Anoth. And thus began my struggle through sixty-six years of mortal life to regain the simple truth of being that was lost the day I first drew breath here on earth.

◙ ◙ ◙

THE COURSE TAKEN BY this chronicle, necessarily, will never follow the smooth flow of a subtly calculated narrative. I say necessarily because I can only write here what I am able to recall as it happened. For if I were to invent episodes for the sake of the story, I would defeat the only purpose I had in continuing with the original manuscript which was, of course, to establish the mutual identity of Anoth and myself, an identity that can be found only in remembered fact. And because the past is a tangled web of experiences of which but few remain visible, only those that can be clearly seen can be reported truthfully. So, as I continue here, you will see that my findings are limited to those few tangible fragments of a life, or shall I say two lives, that somehow still remain accessible to present touch.

This being the case, I cannot expect my memory to stretch itself out before my inner eye like a well composed landscape. I must approach it with my handful of fragments and piece together whatever semblance of a larger reality can be perceived.

◙ ◙ ◙

ONE PHENOMENON THAT I sharply recall from the days of my early childhood is this: time passed with excruciating slowness. I have heard it often said that time seems hardly to move at all when we are young, that it accelerates as one grows older, and by the time we reach old age its pace has become alarmingly fast. In my own case, the deadly burden of time that moved so slowly was actually the weight of my miserable existence. And this was compounded by a continual anxiety to leap forward through time to those precious moments here and there where a pinch of precious happiness was to be found, like the heavenly sound of a latchkey in the front door. But as the burden increases and the anxiety intensifies, time finally becomes as inert as death.

As you may recall, this was no problem for Anoth in Highbelow. Until, of course, he began the anxious task of hopefully completing the writing he had become involved in. Then time became his nemesis. As a mortal child, and later as a grown man, he continued the struggle that began in his other life: to overcome the deadly affliction known as *looking forward with anxiety*.

◙ ◙ ◙

(notation, December, 1970)
AN ACT OF PEACE

It first happened in a child's struggle to overcome the endless tedium of a rocking, knocking, rolling train trip to Littleton, New Hampshire on an unbearably hot day in the summer of 1911. I was that child, and I was about to reach my sixth birthday on the 27th of July.

The journey had started in Chicago, and my memory is vague until the last hours when passing through New England where the haziness of a distant past clears and emerges with the clarity of a present moment. As I write this, sixty years later, I can still feel the discomfort of my stiffly starched sailor suit and black patent-leather shoes. The windows of the coach are open, and the sultry air blows through the soot-laden car. The plush green seats around me are empty, save for those occupied by the enormous bulk and sweaty smell of the governess who is not a human being, but an image of terror and hatred to the two children in her charge, my older sister and myself. Curiously, the presence of my sister does not reappear in my memory. Only the wildly swaying, clackety passage of the train through the heat, the horrible, inescapable presence of the woman, and the turmoil of my anxiety to reach the end of this hopelessly endless journey.

It was the desperate quality of my anxiety that I remember with a vividness that has never left me. My frantic will to have done with the present was smashed and smashed again by an overwhelmingly aggressive and immovable monotony. In spite of admonitions to sit down and stay seated, I could not, for the life of me, keep from wandering from one empty seat to another, sitting for a bit and then up again, being thrown from one side of the aisle to the other, defying the woman's anger and knowing, but not much caring, that cruel punishment awaited me somewhere in that impossible future beyond this endlessness where there would be no prying eyes of strangers to restrain her. Frantically, I willed to be no one, to be nowhere, to leave my skin and this unbearable journey for any tangible destination. The one I had been promised, the summer place near the mountain, I had long ceased to believe in. The future, with its life-affirming sense of desirable expectatio, had vanished. What was left of the world of here and now was a frightening, all enveloping emptiness. The compulsion to escape the terror of this emptiness propelled me toward any action that would confirm the persistence of existence as I had known it. Heedlessly, I provoked the wrath of the woman by climbing in and out of empty seats and challenging the lurching train with sorties down the aisle, inviting the falls, bumps, and bruises that ensued. My anxiety enveloped me like a dense fog. The memory of this painfully corrosive agitation seems to blot out all else, even the beastly anger of the governess, which I must surely have aroused, but which remains on the fringes of my recollection.

How did the miraculous transformation, the act of peace, take place? My memory suddenly finds me quietly sitting, yes peacefully sitting, upright in a huge, hard, scratchy seat, my eyes restfully staring through the window at a swiftly moving conglomeration of passing objects.

What happened? I cannot say for sure. The actual transmutation from one state of being to another is lost to me. I am only vividly aware of living through two lives on that train, one incredibly replacing the other, and both as fresh to my awareness as the sound of my pencil scratching this succession of words across a yellow pad.

Why have I searched out this long-ago experience? Perhaps to rediscover the power of a child to heal himself with his own kind of self-made inner peace. Perhaps without knowing it, I have been looking back to the lost genius of childhood for the final fulfillment that seems beyond the rational grasp of the adult mind. How did this child find his way out of his despair into a world of quiet serenity? Can this lost moment ever be recaptured and relived?

If the child grown old and articulate in his seat at the window on the train could speak, perhaps he would say . . .

"All your life you have been moving away from the truth that was yours to begin with, moving away from it in the persisting hope of finding it somewhere in the passage of time, just beyond the elusive reality of now. Now and now again. Now, now, now, each monotonously ticked off like the idiotic clacking of steel wheels turning on steel rails going nowhere. Now is a lie. You discovered this as a child when you suddenly found timeless, absolute reality, without past or future.

Relive, if you can, the self-consuming sense of joyous peace that came to the child when somehow he saw through the lie, turned from it and, for a few precious moments, found the truth of being. How did it happen? It began with the eyes, remember? The anxious life lives in the past and future, and the Inner Eye that charts the way through memory and expectation cannot function without stealing the sight of the Seeing Eye and blinding it to the visible presence through which it moves. The child's eyes lost their blindness when his wishful memories and anticipations collapsed under the force of hopeless circumstance. And as he looked up and outward he came alive and his being merged with what he saw. Time vanished, and passing moments became visible realities that cluster and collect and endure like the fields and hedges and telephone poles that filled his quiet, eager eyes."

What have I learned from the child? This: Look neither back nor ahead—look only outward. Look long and silently. This is the primal act of peace, like the visual meditation of a painter uniting his painted particles into an enduring presence that will remain perpetually here and now, without beginning or end.

▣ ▣ ▣

THE FOREGOING NOTATION was written before I had made the discovery of my Highbelovian origins. There is now no question but that the phenomenal transmutation that took place on the train was the first time in this life that I was able to regain, if only for a brief few moments, the quiet heart, the open eye, and the contented mind of my former Highbelovian self. Also, it is now obvious that when, years later, as a painter my eyes became obsessed with the miraculous reality of painted surfaces, I was again reaching for the same timeless world that I had discovered at the window on that dusty train.

◨◩◨

(notation, July, 1968)

My obsession on Cape Cod centers in color association—the sun on the pond at various times of the day, the fantastic dark colors of the night, the black-blues and black-greens and black-grays, and above all, the moods of the day persisting into the evening, and evening into night so that you get a kind of twenty-four hour simultaneity. The rising sun is indeed the setting sun, all within one never-beginning, never-ending extended moment. The visible tangibility of the whole twenty-four hours gives a new timelessness to everything and is reassuring.

Although I've never thought of this phenomenon in words until now, I've known that my Cape Cod paintings reach for it. They don't describe. In their own terms, with light and color, they are icons to the experience I've tried to put in words here. Midnight and midday combine into a single visual unity. Stopping the senselessness of time as a past memory or a future anticipation. Stopping the procession of here-now—now-gone moments, making them persist together in a marvelously alive, extended instant of unity. Monet had to paint a dozen paintings at different times of the day. I'm trying to do it with one.

◨◩◨

I HOPE THAT THE READER will bear with the chronological absurdities that I fear will characterize this book. But I am too obsessed with the panoramic unities and continuities of two worlds and two lives to care much whether deeply related events follow one upon the other, or are separated by years. At this juncture, I have no reason to say more about painting, although I am sure I will at some point return to it.

Perhaps the reader will find what seems at times to be a striking identity between his own vaguely remembered childhood experiences and those recorded here. The search for answers to life's age-old puzzlements begins at birth and continues only as long as the child has the freedom of mind and spirit to pursue it. This freedom seldom is permitted to flourish beyond the stage of infancy when insights born of wordless silence and all-seeing eyes are overwhelmed by the mechanics of the imposed behavioral imperatives of the adult world. This is everyone's fate, although we sometimes recognize mutually shared insights recovered from the limbo of our infancy and early childhood. Perhaps you have already found echoes of your own experience in what I have been recounting. If so, I can think of no better reason for continuing with what I've begun.

◧◩◪

FOR AS LONG AS I CAN REMEMBER, I have been deeply curious and greatly puzzled as to what in truth was the precise essence of self — not only within the boundaries of my own existence, but beyond it. And, curiously enough, I have always looked for the answer in phenomena to be seen and found in the world before my eyes rather than inward where one would expect to start such a search. My first remembered encounter with the question of what, for want of a better word I can only call I-ness, was possibly around the age of six or seven. I cannot recall the exact circumstances, but I remember sitting on a doorstep and looking at my hands. What followed was an adventure of the mind that must have impressed me deeply, for it has always come back to haunt me from time to time throughout the years. In August 1966, I finally made the following notation:

> What I have to say here has no source beyond my own existence, pretends to no knowledge beyond my own knowingness, and is concerned with no one's enlightenment but my own.
>
> First, there is a question to ask and answer: Why do I write at all? Why do I expose this world of self to the hazards of communicable language? Words are here and gone, things alien to the timeless inner silence where past existence persists in pure and vivid form, cleansed of identity. One does not write for others from this realm. One writes to find one's way through one's own everlasting continuum. Words are enemies and at the same time saviors. They are asked to identify the unidentifiable without destroying it. Finally, the survival of self depends upon them. For without words, the vast stillness of knowing becomes the silence of oblivion.
>
> How does one speak without breaking the stillness? How simple to paint without disturbing it. But can one speak?
>
> How can it be said? A long ago existence persists. The revelation of the child is the revelation of the man. It persists. But it can be cruelly

suppressed and crippled by the maturing mind. To grow up is to grow away from truth until the understanding, the awareness, the truth that was at the child's fingertips is out of reach.

When I paint I am closer to the child than to the man. Not to his innocence, but to his incomparable insights. Language has become a barrier to the pure knowledge, the revelatory, wordless thought of the child of eight.

That long ago moment of insight persists. It is not recaptured from the past. It is as vividly here and now as it was then. I ask the fingernail of the thumb on my left hand—not any fingernail, but that particular one—I ask it with my eyes glued to it, with all my awareness absorbed by it, I ask, "What are you? What is it to be a fingernail? I, the fingernail. My fingernail must have I-ness just as I have. Does the fingergail have parts as I have? I have a nose, toes, hair, ears. But I am not my nose or toes or ears. When I say *I*, what do I mean? What would it feel like to be a fingernail? I, Robert Wolff, and I, Fingernail. What is I? There is really nothing that I can say is I. I can't touch *I* the way *I* can touch my fingernail. My fingernail is itself just as I am myself. The difference is that my fingernail is something but the *I* of me is nothing, nothing that can be seen or touched.

The child was frightened and bewildered as he entered this anonymous realm, this unidentifiable existence, this vast selflessness.

As the years passed, he learned to cherish this world of spirit. He found here the life-sustaining power of music, of light and color, and a presence as anonymous as himself and his paintings but, unlike himself or his paintings, universal.

▣▣▣

CURIOUSLY, THE SEARCH for a tangible self-identity has always turned outward to discover the I-ness of things beyond the self. I have never gotten over the squeamish horror of stepping on a bug to get rid of it. As a boy I could not do this without shuddering. In later life the act continues, in a lesser way, to disturb me.

(notation, circa 1930)

One is inclined to attribute the way one flinches in stamping out the life of a bug to soft-heartedness. This is a charitable explanation of what, in truth, is a self-concerned horror at being squashed to death under one's own foot.

�(«◻◻»)

BUT ARE WE NOT ALWAYS transferring our sense of I-ness to other things? This is not the self-enclosed subjectivity that turns inward upon itself. It is another kind of subjectivity that releases self and transfers one's own sense of being to the other-ness of what is seen and touched. Whatever cannot be confronted in this way cannot ever be fully known. Objective knowledge often lacks this knowingness and thus limits the actual experiencing of truth to conceptual intangibles, remote from self. Out of this frustration, I once reached for thunder:

(notation, circa 1935)

Is it not strange that such a cataclysm as thunder in the sky should come to me as a mere noise in my ears?

◻◻◻

THE I OF OTHER PEOPLE

(notation, London, 1927)

Tonight as I opened the door a cab went by and the cabman was singing. For one instant, my surroundings, instead of strange, seemed familiar.

◻◻◻

THE EXTENSION OF SELF into the being of another is the basis of human understanding. The hostile world in which Miss Bowman isolated me had no place for this kind of perceptive give and take. As a consequence, I can remember having no friends my own age and no sense of human kinship to people in general, starting with the symbolic inhumanity of the woman herself. I can imagine no one with a greater sense of aloneness than the one I carried with me the first day I was deposited at school and left there surrounded by a room full of children.

I had just turned six and I was filled with the misgivings of one who had never been given a reason to trust whatever confronted him from beyond his own barricaded existence. At school, I dared not step from behind that barricade and though I caused little trouble, I made no friends. I was quiet and went about my business while the other children, as I recall, tolerated my aloofness by ignoring me. What impressed me most about those first days at school was not the children nor the teacher nor the new surroundings, but the absence of Miss Bowman. My greatest desire was to attract as little attention as possible. When I was called upon to speak my throat closed upon any words I tried to utter. I learned to read and write quite readily, but I was a slow-minded student and lagged behind the others in the race to keep up with the tasks and assignments that were given us.

When I look back upon those first years at school, I do not recall any special interests or pleasures. I saw the schoolroom as principally a haven of refuge from my life at home. I tried to do what I was told. The only reprimands that I drew seem to have been constant admonitions to stop dreaming and pay attention to what the teachers were saying. I was very bored, for the most part, and time passed slowly. I did not mind this too much, but rather found a certain comfort in the endless days. I was shy if not a bit fearful toward my classmates and although I made no friends I was less wary of the girls than the boys. For the boys were inclined to tease me, which always angered me and intensified my feelings of beleaguered isolation. From the very first, I was aware of being different from everyone around me. I envied the others, their easy intimacy, their games, shouts, friendships and loyalties. Yet, I was so hopelessly estranged that I never tried to join them.

There was one horrible day I shall never forget. It was a Wednesday in second grade. Wednesday was the day when, after school, I would have to hurry home ("Do not linger on the way, Robert, or you'll be sorry!") because of dancing school. Usually, I would rush into the house and change from my school clothes to the white sailor suit with the white stockings and black patent leather dancing pumps. However, on this particular Wednesday, for some reason that involved Miss Bowman's convenience, I was forced to go to school in my dancing school clothes. I remember pleading with her not to do this to me. For such a costume was outlandishly taboo among the children. Worst of all were the white stockings, which on a boy somehow symbolized everything he should not be. I don't know how I managed to run the gamut of jibes and insults but in looking back I find myself frozen with mortification, seated at my usual desk in the classroom as the teacher conducts the lesson from the front of the room. There is some significance in the fact that she is the only grown person in my eight years in that school that vividly comes to life in my memory. She was a thin, kindly looking woman with red hair and her name was Miss O'Brian.

I remember enduring the suppressed whispers and laughter of the boys seated around me until my torture became unbearable and I rushed from the class to the cloakroom, where I hid my face in the cluster of coats and hats and tried to choke back the sobs that overwhelmed me.

Then, for the first time in my short life, I felt the consoling comfort of encircling arms and a soft voice to help me through a moment of hopelessness and defeat. Through my tears, I saw the sweet face of Miss O'Brian as she asked me to tell her what the trouble was. And I remember how, gradually, the blind hysteria left me, and how I managed to tell her about the hated costume that was meant for dancing school. I recall the reassuring way she told me to try to ignore the other children. There must have been other wise things she said, because after what seemed a very long time, we both emerged from the dressing room with my face dry and my head held high. I returned to my seat and no one took notice, except one girl who leaned over from her desk across from mine with some reassuring, whispered words that lifted my spirits.

There is one thing more to be said about this episode: I am certain that, even with the sympathetic encouragement of the teacher to confide in, I did not tell on Miss Bowman. I did not even mention her name. And if I did, it was not to blame her.

◙ ◙ ◙

IN THE SUMMER OF 1955, I was invited to Madison, Wisconsin to spend a week as Visiting Artist at the University. I had known that the assignment also involved a visit to the University's summer art school outside Madison, but was surprised to find upon my arrival in Madison that I would be revisiting Madeleine Island in the far north. I had not been there since I was a boy of eight, forty-two years before.

My sister, who as a child suffered from hay fever, required a northern climate each summer where she could escape the pollen-infested cities of the central plains. Starting with our summer in New Hampshire, Miss Bowman would take us each year to a different locale, always at some distant northern point. We never, as I remember, returned to the same place, a fact which I am inclined to attribute to the woman's caution not to expose her child-rearing methods to public view for any protracted period of time at any one given place.

Madeleine Island was reached by a ferry boat from the mainland, as is still the case. I have always remembered the large sprawling building that extended along the shore and the long landing wharf that led up from the water across the beach directly to the entrance of the hotel. I remember the weathered look of the place, a huge, simple structure of unpainted, seasoned boards with that special quality of hardy flimsiness found in very old summer places that have survived the years of hot weather habitation and long winters of disuse. There was also a special musty smell about the place that I loved and would sniff at like a puppy dog after a favorite scent.

Behind the hotel at one end, a pine-covered hill extended back for some distance to a flat clearing in the forest where two tennis courts sat. I do not remember actually playing tennis, but I vividly recall the path that wound through weeds and trees leading from the hotel to the courts. I used that path often. One day in particular deeply affected my life.

I have recorded this episode elsewhere (*On Art and Learning*. Grossman Publishers: New York, 1971.) but I return to it here in greater detail because it has always remained one of my most treasured experiences. As I started up the path that day, nothing specific was occupying my thoughts. I can only remember a sense of aimless empty-headedness as my eyes examined the weeds that lined the path, then the path itself, and finally fixed upon my bare feet as one replaced the other in my forward movement up the hill. I remember the feeling of being blissfully alone without a thought in my head, contentedly absorbing every random stimulus that happened to touch my senses.

Then suddenly, as my right foot came forward to meet the ground, I saw a small piece of white birch bark lying exactly where I was about to step. The longest, most enduring instant of my life ensued, an interval of time that is the nearest thing to eternity that I or anyone else will ever experience. During the time that intervened between the first sight of the target and the felt pressure of my foot as I stepped upon it, I promised myself that I would keep this instant alive forever, that I would never forget it. If anyone had been watching me, he would have seen a small boy walking steadily up the path without breaking the rhythm of his stride. I did not stop or turn around to examine the bark or to ponder what had happened. I knew that whatever it was, I was taking it with me and that I would have it for all time. I do not remember reaching the tennis courts, but I presume I did.

On my first visit to Madison in 1955 when my hosts first told me of the plan to spend a few days at the summer school on Madeleine Island, the mere mention of the name produced a memory response that was as clear and immediate as the day before yesterday. However, because I was finding little to interest me in the discursive tasks expected of a visiting artist, and because I was certain that there would be little left on the island that I would remember, I was not anxious to make the trip.

We motored from Madison in an overcrowded sedan, and the limits of polite conversation were exhausted long before the five- or six-hour trip was over. When we finally reached the landing of the ferry that would take us to our final destination, I was thoroughly depressed, a mood hardly becoming a guest of honor. I stood alone at the bow of the ferry and watched the distant shore as it gradually diminished, until the trees and buildings, and then people could no longer be made out. Finally we approached a long wharf that extended a hundred feet or more out from the shore. As I stepped off the boat and followed the others down the length of the wharf I realized at once that I was no stranger to this place. For there was the old, rambling, rickety summer hotel, fronted by a white beach and silhouetted from behind by a hill of brush topped by tall pines almost exactly as I had left it forty-six years before.

I made an effort once or twice during the next two days to fill the increasingly large conversation gaps with references to my early visit to the island when the school building was a summer hotel. I never could bring myself to mention my adventure on the hill any more than could I, for some remote reason, persuade myself to re-explore the path that led up to the tennis courts. Upon asking, I was told that the courts were still there. I was unbelieving, but I left the island without climbing the hill to see for myself.

◙◙◙

As the days dragged on through the first years of Miss Bowman's rule, I became more and more obsessed with the perverse immobility of time. Prison inmates must suffer the same frustration. For the more one longs for a liberating future, the further away it seems to move, and the successive tickings of the clock, supposedly moving forward in time, become a mockery. When time in this way seems to stand still, the sense of the present becomes intolerable. My first remembered struggle with this phenomenon took place on the train trip to which I have already referred. There I learned that the present is destroyed by the delusion of a future that remains endlessly out of reach. What I learned, of course, was immediately forgotten, but my obsession to turn from the emptiness of tomorrow to the touch of the present haunted me in those early years and still is with me.

(notation, undated)

Hurry through the present and you will never find the past.

◙◙◙

It seems now that I must have been plagued with the question, "When is Now?" from the moment I was born. There must have been many confrontations with the problem although only a few remain clear. I know that at a certain age, somewhere around eight or nine, I challenged the ephemeral movement of time by trying to extend the sound of a finger snapping to make it exist long enough to call it a *now* (mentioned in *On Art and Learning*). I would snap my fingers, one snap slowly following another, successively giving each a greater and greater auditory effort, as though permanency could be achieved by a powerful will to stretch the duration of each sound as it occurred. Frustrated, I would shorten the intervals between the snaps and make them, one after the other, come faster and faster so as to bring them all together into a sound that would last long enough to be called now before it disappeared. Naturally I was constantly defeated by the futility of trying to design permanency into the present, or even to find an extra instant of duration. I know I never actually believed that I might succeed, but I couldn't resist the temptation to try over and over again. I vaguely remember being questioned about my strange preoccupation when someone, I do not know who, surprised me one day in the act of endlessly snapping my fingers. I did not dare reveal my purpose for fear of being laughed at.

回 回 回

(notation, 1927)
PAST, PRESENT AND FUTURE

Perhaps a sundial, with all its limitations, told time better than our modern clocks do. Though it did not tell the hour to the second, at least it let the hour endure. Our clock chops up the hour into infinity. And so, instead of just letting us **be** as the sundial did, the clock divides up our lives into a progression of ticks. Instead of letting us live, as the sundial did, the clock reminds us that we are growing old. Should time be silently extended or knick-knockingly told off? The dial does one thing, the clock the other.

THE ARGUMENT AGAINST THE DIAL in favor of the clock is a matter of accuracy. But it is not, as people suppose, an accuracy in regard to time that the clock gives. It is rather an accuracy regarding the division of our lives into dinner engagements and dentist appointments. To time it gives a false sense of fleetingness. On the other hand, the soft shadow that moves across the dial moves imperceptibly like time itself. It does not tell time, it reveals it. The clock actually talks too much to be trusted. While you listen to it, it hammers home its points most convincingly, but when you leave it for the stillness of a vast starry night, you know that you've been taken in.

◫◫◫

(notation, 1930)

The idea that we live from one moment to the next is absurd. Most of us live from the next moment to the one after that.

◫◫◫

(notation, 1931)

Time is immeasurable space and our illusion that it moves is our feeble way of trying to relate our physical world to it. Actually, passing minutes do not exist and are but passing objects in the abstract.

◫◫◫

I AM NOT BY NATURE a superstitious person, although I have always taken due cognizance of experiences that resist rational explanation but yet cannot be brushed aside as oddities of chance or just simple coincidence. Each year, the month of November begins like any other and continues so until, as often is the case, something of special import, for better or worse, takes place. Then suddenly, I awaken to the fact that here again is November with one of its strange surprises, like the one in 1917 when the reign of May Bowman finally came to an end.

Neither my sister nor I had any forewarning that such a great event was about to take place. We did not know the discussions between the woman and my father that no doubt led to the dismissal, if such it was. The first inkling we had of the impending miracle was Miss Bowman coming to us in tears to say she was leaving. And, good reader, believe it or not, I tried with all the might of my make-believe powers to bring tears to my eyes, and failed to make sad sounds that could be mistaken for weeping. Unbelieving, and immediately wary of being tricked, I was careful not to let my guard down, or to allow the slightest flicker of my real feelings to show upon my face. My sister, without prior consultation with me, responded in exactly the same way, and before long we were actually begging the monster not to leave us, hoping against hope that our pleas would go unheeded. Luckily, the decision was irrevocable and nothing we could do or say would change it. But even as she shut the door behind her, we were certain she would soon return. It was several days before we began to suspect that a miracle had actually happened.

And that was the last of Miss Bowman. My sister and I waited several weeks, and then gradually and cautiously told our stories to my father. The poor man at first was incredulous until the evidence became inescapable. The shock and remorse that he must have felt was reflected in his lifelong compulsion thereafter to provide us, as far as he was able, with everything our hearts desired.

PART III

My new freedom brought with it an end to the years of withdrawal and isolation. The old longing to have done with the agonies of this life, to return to that happier existence that I once knew, was gradually dissipated by an eagerness to find a friendlier place in my immediate world. Until now, it had seemed closed to me.

This was the beginning of a long period of estrangement from that spirited inner life, that no doubt had its origins in my Highbelovian past and which I now recognize as my most precious possession in this mortal life. I was twelve years-old and in the eighth grade. I enjoyed the prestige of being one of the older students. It was a time of growing self-assurance, and I remember making special efforts not to appear different in any way from my contemporaries but to act and think as everyone else did.

◧ ◧ ◧

(notation, circa 1955)

I love the sight of things.
Not telescopically,
Not microscopically,
Not in motion
Cinematically,
'Nor frozen photographically.

Not to have
Or have not.
Not to study.
Not to hoard.
I mean,
No dappled wings
Pinned to a board.
I mean,
I love the sight of things.

◻◻◻

I HAD ALWAYS BEEN somewhat ashamed of my low grades at school and had envied the esteem that came to my more clever and persevering school-mates. Yet, I was not concerned enough to generate the driving effort it would have taken to improve my grades. In class, I spent most of my time in dreamy, open-eyed concentration on whatever I found to gaze at: white clouds in a blue sky framed by the large classroom windows, the silky, golden hair of a certain girl or the pattern and colors of her dress, the cast of a certain face or the motion of the teacher's hand as I ignored the meaning of a notation she would scrawl across the blackboard. The sheer act of looking and seeing never bored me, while the words and numbers that came from books were met by a blank and unresponsive mind.

There was perhaps one exception. It seems that I was fascinated by the di-agrams and maps that filled my geography book. For one day I found myself released from the usual classroom activities for the purpose of reproducing a large wall map of the United States. I do not remember any previous interest in drawing nor of anyone noticing any ability I might have shown. As far as I can recall, there were no school activities involving drawing or painting. Perhaps the teacher discovered a natural gift for drawing in the quality of the maps I produced for her geography assignments. No doubt, she decided that a large, accurately drawn wall map would be helpful in teaching geog-raphy. And perhaps there was also the thought that here at last was some-thing for me to do that at least was more productive than my incorrigible habit of daydreaming.

I have no clear recollection of the exact details of the project, but certain aspects of the experience do remain vivid. The drawing surface was a large rectangular sheet of white paper, possibly five feet long, which was mounted at the end of the blackboard that extended along one wall of the room. I remember standing there with a book in one hand and a piece of crayon in the other, and without further preparation transferring the lines of the map exactly as I found them in the book, proportioned to the precise scale required to fill the white paper's expanse. I knew no tricks, such as grids, that mural painters have used for centuries to transfer their small preparatory drawings to great expanses of wall. I remember having no misgivings about the ultimate success of my efforts. I went about my task with enormous pleasure and for the first time in my life, with a happy sense of pride in excelling in work of value to others.

As I consider how recklessly I went about the construction of this map with nothing but the naked eye to guide my hand in the exacting problems of proportion and size, direction and placement of lines, and other details, I am filled with wonder at the innocent skill of a twelve year-old lad for having actually succeeded with a method that more experienced hands would hardly dare attempt. I worked slowly, for I was under no pressure to hurry to a finish. And being free of the daily class work that bored me so, I felt no inclination to speed things up. As the days passed, I became more and more engrossed in the image that was gradually emerging. I became so completely absorbed that when at the end of the day I was brought back to reality and told that it was time to go home, it was like waking from a dream.

In this way, the work went on for several weeks. In fact, I became so involved in perfecting every detail of the drawing that the teacher finally had to pronounce the map finished and order me back to my desk. It was like a disagreeable awakening from a delightful dream.

(notation, November, 1952)

To paint is to accustom yourself to such a brilliant light that you run the risk of blinding yourself in all other things—like going from the sun into a darkened room.

🔲 🔲 🔲

(notation, circa 1938)

Words are symbols of doubt; color and form of faith.

🔲 🔲 🔲

I HAD TO SUFFER five more years of unrelieved scholastic verbiage before I had another brief opportunity to exercise the keen but undernourished sensory intelligence that provided my eighth-grade classroom with what I am sure was a truly remarkable map of the United States. The schools I attended followed educational principles that assumed that a focused open eye was a reflection of a closed mind, that the senses were contrasted to the intellect as purgatory to paradise, and the work of the hands was a poor thing compared to the findings of the mind. Sensory intelligence might be an admissible attribute of the beasts but was of no consequence to a civilized young fellow seeking a civilized education. The only exercise my starved sensory faculties received throughout seven years of secondary school and college was romping in gymnasiums and doodling graffiti in the margins of my textbooks. For four long years, I attended highly respectable preparatory schools with highly respectable academic curricula designed to enrich the empty minds and suppress the natural sensibilities of young men preparing for four more years of an even higher form of brain stuffing known as a college education.

My scholarly abilities and inclinations being what they were, the reader will wonder how the guardians of academic excellence at Yale University were persuaded to admit anyone with a scholastic record as sorry as mine. My induction into the freshman class in 1923 was an entirely fortuitous event arising out of an act of revenge perpetrated without the faintest trace of an educational motive. For three unbelievable years I was to wander about the beautiful New Haven campus in a state of comatose wonderment at the miraculous absurdity of my presence there.

How did it come about? The propelling power was pure hatred, the object of which was a harmless, well-manicured fellow who taught English at the preparatory school I'd attended. One winter, five months before I was scheduled to graduate along with the rest of the boys in the room, Mr. Kirk, as I shall call him, asked each of us what college we had chosen to enter in the fall. One by one, the answers were given including institutions of the highest academic standing starting with Harvard. I listened with certain awe to the confident, matter-of-fact way that each boy indicated his choice. Because my name was last on Mr. Kirk's list by reason of an alphabetic if not academic order, I had plenty of time to consider the matter and make up my mind. I had no idea what made one institution preferable to another, so I based my decision on the fact that three of the most likable boys in the room had chosen Yale. Finally when it came my turn, Mr. Kirk gave me a level look tinged with disgust and said, "And now what about you, Wolff?"

In a voice as casual and unconcerned as I could command, I softly spoke the word *Yale*. Mr. Kirk raised his pretty eyebrows and slowly informed me, to the vast amusement of everyone, that when I entered Yale he would enter heaven. I had no idea how I would manage it but then and there I swore to myself that nothing could keep me out of Yale or from the pleasure of opening the pearly gates for this son-of-a-bitch.

◧◧◧

(notation, 1928)

There is nothing more hopelessly unanswerable than the contempt of a fool.

◧◧◧

I TOOK THE STORY HOME to my father who was delighted that I had at last found a reason, shoddy as it was, for fighting my way into one of the institutions of higher learning. With great good humor he joined in a quest for a way to effect my revenge on Mr. Kirk, and after a considerable time of concentrated research we came up with the Rosenbaum Tutoring School, a small New England institution with a lethal brain and a standing guarantee to squeeze anyone of sound mind and body into the college of his choice within the shortest possible time. Two weeks to the day after Mr. Kirk had thrown out his invidious challenge I arrived in the snow and sleet of a February afternoon at the main building of this incredible enterprise dealing in prescribed knowledge. And here I settled down for the next five months pleasantly imprisoned and well fed, and ceaselessly occupied in a non-stop excursion into rote learning such as I had never dreamed possible.

May I say, at this point, that it is my belief that brain cramming can only succeed as an act of gamesmanship and never as a serious discipline in the pursuit of excellence. For the first time in my life I enjoyed having second-hand, well sorted out and done with knowledge poured into my understanding like wheat into an empty bin, because here at last I had found a motivation which, in its sheer stupidity, matched the perversity of the teaching process itself. During pauses in the struggles of my embattled memory with logarithm tables and quotations from Julius Caesar, I delighted my imagination with vivid images of a visit to Mr. Kirk, seated at his desk, scowling through his fury and frustration as I informed him that I will release him from the absurd bargain that he had made and that instead of going to heaven he could go to hell where he really belonged, while I settled down to the enviable life of a Yale man. What years of teachers' cajoling, pleading, and persuasion could never accomplish was easily achieved by a simple urge to annihilate a hated personality.

This of course, explains why so many simple people have been able to absorb the large quantities of undigested knowledge that goes with a college education. If the motive is simple and compelling enough, like improved social status or a seat on the stock exchange, or even the humiliation of a harmless English teacher, the horrors of a conventional education can be fairly easily overcome. I was able to prove this by passing all my entrance examinations with grades that would have astounded every teacher who heretofore had anything to do with me.

Before leaving this episode, I must record the dismal outcome of my long-anticipated confrontation with Mr. Kirk after being allowed to call myself a Yale man. When I tried to remind him of his insulting challenge he laughed, saying he remembered saying no such thing and changed the subject.

It was in my second year at Yale, when to my utter amazement, the miracle of my eighth grade map was repeated in another guise, this time a biology laboratory.

Two celebrated professors named Woodruff and Baitrell conducted the biology course. Woodruff was a quiet, stolid little man who droned out his lectures in a cadenced monotone which affected me like a lullaby sung to a sleepy baby. At the first few lectures, I tried to find some undiscovered corner of my understanding that would reveal the meaning of the words that marched past my ears in single file, all dressed in the same inflection, one indistinguishable from the other. I soon gave in to the hypnotizing effect that the voice had on my unemployed senses and tended to doze through it all. To do this without fear of detection, I was careful to choose a seat well to the rear of the semi-circular lecture hall which rose steeply row-by-row until those farthest back found themselves looking not at the face but down the bald head of the lecturer.

I slept peacefully through the course save for the time when a fellow sitting next to me jammed his elbow into my ribs and silently held up a small round agate marble which he ostentatiously placed at the edge of the step of our row of seats and then gently pushed it over. It dropped with a sharp metallic *pang* to the next step, rolled forward and dropped again. The verbal droning from down front stopped. The silence in the room seemed more hushed than any silence should be. The good professor looked up and stared at nothing out of the frozen immobility of his expressionless face; he just stood there and waited out the journey of the marble, as one *pang* slowly followed another with a kind of evil monotony, until after an endless interval, it came to rest at his feet. Without comment, he turned back to his notes on the lectern and continued droning as though nothing had happened. My heart filled with a crazy kind of admiration for the man and I remember trying for a time to decipher what he was saying but soon gave up. It goes without saying that I eventually flunked his half of the course.

The other half, Baitrell's half, was the work in the biology laboratory. I had little to do with Professor Baitrell but remember being helped along by several young assistants. The tasks involved taking dead frogs and other creatures out of ice boxes, slicing them open, and then recording in a large notebook, page after page, the exact appearance of their interiors. For the life of me, I could not bring myself to use the knife on these dead things. By promising to compensate for my squeamish dereliction with the extraordinary efforts I would give to drawing the sickening display, I finally I persuaded one of the assistants to perform the surgery for me. And sickening it was. The smell of formaldehyde that permeated the laboratory made it all the worse.

However, with a considerable effort of will the image of a cruelly tortured frog, skinned and pinned spread-eagled to a board, gradually transformed itself into a marvelously intricate pattern of lines and shapes and convolutions. What had once been the heart, the liver, brain, organs, and intestines of a mutilated creature dissolved and miraculously reappeared in the fascinating form of a meticulous drawing.

For the remainder of the term, I gave myself over wholly to my exquisite delineations of the little dead things from which I was meant to derive factual knowledge but which for me were nothing more than exercises in sheer visual enjoyment. I amazed my friends by remaining after hours in the laboratory and staying up late at night to perfect the drawings in my notebook. For they mistook my purely sensory compulsion for an extraordinary awakening of heretofore unsuspected scholarly interests. This strange assumption was fortified not only by the exceptional quality of the drawings, but also by the elegant precision of the hand-lettered names and labels that identified the various organs and parts.

While my understanding of biological science was totally unaffected by my laboratory experience, I learned a great deal about the art of drawing. I discovered, for one thing, that a drawing remains a drawing and is never whatever it represented. I found that my eyes absorbed more detail than a good drawing could actually use. And I also found in selecting what should not be drawn that there was the danger of oversimplifying the truth that lay in such profusion under the microscope lens or in view of the naked eye. I became quite expert in finding the middle ground between a simplistic emptiness and an overstuffed naturalism, and my teachers, including the professor in charge, were enchanted with what finally I proudly submitted for evaluation. My notebook was returned marked with an overwhelmingly high grade somewhere in the upper nineties. It was the first and last time I experienced the euphoria of academic stardom. It did not, however, persuade whoever calculated my final biology grade that I had done anything extraordinary. He was insensitive enough to flunk me.

◙◙◙

(notation, circa 1932)

It is not drawing from what you see, but from what you have looked at that counts.

◙◙◙

("TOWARD A DIRECT VISION," FROM THE CATALOGUE OF THE SECOND ANNUAL EXHIBITION OF THE AMERICAN ABSTRACT ARTISTS, 1938)

When I paint I am moved by a plastic experience. When I look at the everyday world I experience visual emotions. If I should try to represent what I see I should have to favor one aspect for its plastic possibilities as against another with no such possibilities. In doing this I force the world about me, from which I draw my vitality, into special aspects. My visual contact with it becomes arbitrary and subject to the limitations of my decisions as to what I can and cannot paint.

For example, I see the vista of the city with its lights and electric signs moving swiftly through the shifting spaces of night. If to paint is to describe and represent, then I am forced to reject this experience because it will not submit to plastic analysis. This self-imposed blindness cuts off the artist from those great visual events which the world is seeing for the first time. He escapes into the security of those restricted aspects of the contemporary world that can still be compressed into the pictorial conception. The artless layman, living in visual freedom, in the end will live a broader visual life than this painter.

The contemporary painter cannot combine representation with direct and simple plastics. We cannot call from the past the archaic mind and eye as readily as the archaic form. The eyes of contemporary man see with an inherent microscopic naturalism. He fools himself who thinks he can represent contemporary life and at the same time achieve authentic simplicity by means of a process of elimination. In doing this the painter, above all, eliminates his own real self.

Apply the microscope outside, everywhere and anywhere. It is undeniably ours. Why make an encumbrance of it by first limiting its scope in the name of descriptive art and then throwing out all but the fragments of its findings in the name of simplicity? This is to transform a priceless faculty into an instrument of escape. Let it reveal its wonders and let us absorb its revelations. But let us not resort to aesthetic hieroglyphics in a desperate effort to give these revelations to "art." Accept the camera. It will do the job easily and beautifully.

We must forget art biases and absorb direct, uncatalogued experience. The painter looks at everything. He rejects nothing. He cannot be visually predisposed for or against. He must not drag into the studio favorite odds and ends of the world outside. His canvas must be another and independent visual experience. In this way only will he achieve a plastic vision that will be of this and not of a bygone world. A direct vision.

◧◧◧

THE BIOLOGY LABORATORY and my eighth grade classroom provided the only nourishment my neglected Highbelovian intelligence and talent were to find throughout the fifteen years of formal education that was meant to make a cultured man of me. My studies were not ever tainted with utilitarian purposes either in preparing me for useful work involving the eyes and hands or some kind of commercial enterprise. I listened to lectures and read books that prescribed how to think and feel about the art, literature, poetry and philosophy of the ages and then I was obliged to repeat what I had been told in written tests that reassured the teacher of his own erudition and celebrated the emptiness of his own mind. How I managed to make myself tolerable to the school authorities still makes me wonder. My scholastic standing was always on the brink of total failure, yet I managed, incredible as it now seems, to escape dismissal.

My revulsion against the force feeding of knowledge was as strong as my distaste for the food Miss Bowman once shoved down my throat. At nineteen, the college lecture room invoked the same dream-like inattention that the schoolroom did as a small boy. However, following the reawakening of my numbed sensibilities in the biology laboratory, I discovered that the vital organs of frogs were not the only source of visual interest that could be transformed into artifacts. After years of staring blankly at the backs of students seated around me in classrooms, one day, in the midst of a philosophy lecture, they all appeared to me as a structured conglomeration of beautifully configured lines. Then and there the erudite voice intoning its half-heard verbal abstractions was silenced and I began to draw again.

As I wandered in and out of one classroom after another, I filled my notebooks with linear aspects of the arms, heads, shoulders, and backs of my classmates, seated and slouched in a variety of positions and postures. In each case the special character of outlines and contours combined into a linear image that precisely identified the particular human condition that until then was just another no one, shrouded in anonymity.

One boy would sit slouched with an arm stretched out along the back of the seat next to him as though ready to pillow the head that drooped over it. Then there was the tense erect figure anxiously leaning forward in a body gesture that, in a few penciled lines, told more about the boy's academic worries and ambitions than a page full of words could. A propped head, slightly sagging as the supporting hand and arm slowly gave way, until, as sleep took over, the head fell forward with a startled jerk. And of course there was always one blissfully relaxed figure sleeping unashamedly, head resting on chest, both arms stretched over the backs of the adjacent seats to keep the limp body from sliding to the floor.

I must hasten to explain that I had no interest (and, of course, no skill) in rendering anatomical detail or facial likenesses. I was fascinated simply by the sort of lines and contours that would flow and curve and suddenly stop and turn and then go on, to end in a penciled embodiment of a certain movement or gesture. I delighted in these drawings even though I put no more value on them than the people around me would have, thinking of them as perhaps a silly but pleasant distraction in an otherwise boring situation. Today I dearly wish that I had saved a few, because I am sure they would reveal to me certain fresh insights that my now more sophisticated eye fails to invoke.

Ironically, I made some of my best scribblings from the top row of the lecture hall where an extremely dull course in the History of Art was given. And though I wasn't completely bored like I was in most of my other subjects, the purely aesthetic pleasure I derived from my drawings seemed to have nothing in common with the subject matter which consisted of chronological listings of names, dates, and places, together with lifeless lantern slides and reproductions. The materialistic culture in which I had grown up had held no place for art, and although I had been given the benefit of two summer sight-seeing tours of Europe with the usual museum visits, I came to the art history course almost a complete innocent. What puzzles me today is how a course study dealing with man's greatest visual achievements could fail to elicit from a young fellow as visually endowed as I was no more than a mere willingness to memorize the scholarly facts that were thrust at him. It wasn't until two years after I left Yale that I discovered the thrill of seeing a great painting come alive before my eyes. It happened in London on one of many leisurely visits to the National Gallery in the Turner room. But that is something else again.

My aversion to the purely verbal aspects of my education was not as total as perhaps I have made it seem. After all, I was assigned textbooks and reading references, and while my response in terms of studious effort was minimal, I did what I considered was an abnormal amount of reading and writing. Not all of this was involuntary. In my sophomore year I began to read, haphazardly to be sure, books of my own choosing covering a diversity of authors and subjects that far exceeded the limits of my required reading. And I began to give word to my own thoughts, timidly at first, on scraps of paper. Then, as I gained respect for the forbidden independence of my own mind, I started a notebook. This was in no sense a diary. For I found no reason to verbally inflate the unremarkable daily routine of college life. No, my compulsion to write was not a born fascination with my own words and word images. I did not (and still do not) enjoy writing. I turned to writing because in the course of my uneventful young life, certain perceptions and observations arising out of daily circumstances refused simply to pass through my understanding like birds in flight but remained in the front of my mind to hound my conscience until I confirmed their identity with words. In this way, my notebook became a sort of permanent shelter for vague insights where a passing thought might linger and be strengthened and with luck might reach for revelation. When this happened, my impatience with words vanished and I accepted their magic with a certain helpless awe. I never seemed to master the art of writing, then or now. It rather, at times, seemed to master me.

I was twenty years-old and I remember being hounded by the absurd discrepancy between the precise orderliness of academic reality and my own chaotically unpredictable existence. I could never reconcile the haphazard nature of cause and effect that from day to day determined not only the course of my own existence but also that of society in general, with the everything-in-its-place orderliness of the learned world of textbooks and professors. And so, one day, I opened my notebook and flung back at my teachers all their well-tempered certitudes with the following notation which, while it might not charm the reader, was for me truly memorable:

> Looking back gives an inevitable twist to a series of events, each of which at the time of incident was seeking an uncertain outcome. A review of these events, viewed as a series, consequently will make life seem more ordered and inevitable and less adventurous and uncertain than it really is.

Two years later, after absorbing the subjective and wondrously humanistic view of evolution found in the works of Samuel Butler and Henri Bergson, I added the following note:

> Herein lies the Darwinian omission that Butler pointed out and Bergson endeavored to supply.

回回回

I DO NOT REMEMBER much about the various courses I took, most of which I was obliged to choose for one official reason or another. By the time I reached my junior year one course seemed to me very much like the next. For although there was a diversity of subjects, they all seemed to inhabit the same intellectual prison. It would be too easy to attribute my disenchantment to a youthful rebellion against doing what I was told to do instead of being allowed to go about things in my own way. I would surely have been capable of learning from others had that learning catalyzed rather than suppressed my inclination, fragile and immature as it was, to think for myself.

There was, however, one exception among my many courses where, for once, students were given an opportunity to read and explore and draw their own conclusions before the professor would allow his own views and interpretations to be heard. The course was extremely popular because of the professor's genial personality and the casual way he conducted class. He was, in fact, somewhat of a campus joke, not too greatly respected by his colleagues. Every term his classes, which met in a larger lecture hall, were oversubscribed. I managed somehow to be admitted in my junior year.

The course was known as Contemporary Drama and was given by the famous William Lyon (Billy) Phelps. There were always overtones of the matinee idol in the affable egotism that brightly colored his classroom performance, as evidenced by his popularity as a speaker at literary afternoons of ladies' clubs. His lectures wandered aimlessly from one topic to another and seldom remained centered on the subject at hand. Each week, we were assigned a play to read and a paper to write, giving our opinions of what we had read. When he wished to make his own comments he would, as likely as not, choose one of the student reports which appealed to him and read it aloud to convey his approved view of the matter. He managed, in this way, never to speak too long on the subject of contemporary drama before switching to his inexhaustible collection of stories and anecdotes which included everything from a favorite cooking recipe to a walking tour of the hill towns of Italy. To me he was a wonderful old fellow and I enjoyed his course immensely. He even surprised me one day by reading aloud from my paper on Gogol's Lower Depths. I did not wake up to the sound of my own words until he had almost finished with the page, but I became so inflated with the euphoria of discovering that someone had given credence to thoughts that were my very own that I did not hear a word of the remainder of the lecture.

It seems a pity that no one took the dear man seriously. If he did nothing else, he made his students assume responsibility for their own judgments and opinions. And in the academic world of 1925, this seems to have been a rarity. Of course, my limited schedule of courses could not include numbers of well known scholars who might have surprised me had I known them, and perhaps it is time to concede the probability that there were at least a few who would have.

However, I am not forgetting that I became a Yale undergraduate almost by accident and that my right to judge my mentors will surely be questioned. By the time I reached my junior year, my efforts to conform to the rules and standards of academic excellence were dissipated by my boredom with formal class work and a growing enthusiasm for many new and self-discovered interests. I began to frequent the New Haven bookstores and absorb more and more books of my own choosing with time stolen from my required studies. I enjoyed the freedom to discard any book that bored me without finishing it and to re-read the revelations and discoveries in those that I cherished. Soon I began to acquire a preference for special writers and developed the habit of discovering where their minds met on shared views and perceptions. One after the other, I came upon Anatole France, Bernard Shaw, Dostoevsky, Samuel Butler, Jacob Wasserman, Chekov, Turgenev and others. I went into debt buying a thirty volume set of the complete works of France and I read everything I could find of Shaw and Butler who became my special heroes. My notebook, which had begun timidly and tentatively, began to fill with my own fragile observations and conclusions. And the most curious part of this intellectual self-awakening,

LEGACY
SUNSET AT LONG POND

a poem by
WENDY WOLFF BLUMBERG

My Father's long fingers
Hold the brush again
They move across the canvas
In their own rhythm
Paint the sun coral
As it goes down
Turn it to rust under the water
Against blue of night
Against the blue of Long Pond
Cold   deep
In the light that remains

This belongs to me, I tell him
It belongs to you, he finally agrees

In the studio at Wellfleet
At the edge of the dune
We can smell the ocean
Through the open top of the Dutch door
He steps back from the easel
To study this painting
That has come to me
When he dies

Aaron Wolff, Robert's father 1868 — 1928

R.J.W., circa 1918

R.J.W. and sister, Rosina

R.J.W. & first wife, Alice Wolff
(Stine), Paris, circa 1929

In the Navy, circa 1943

R.J.W. & daughter, Wendy, circa 1937

With friend Eddy Ehrich, Fire Island, New
York, circa 1941; young Pete Eising stands
in bottom left corner

"Untitled," 1945, Casein, 23" X 29"

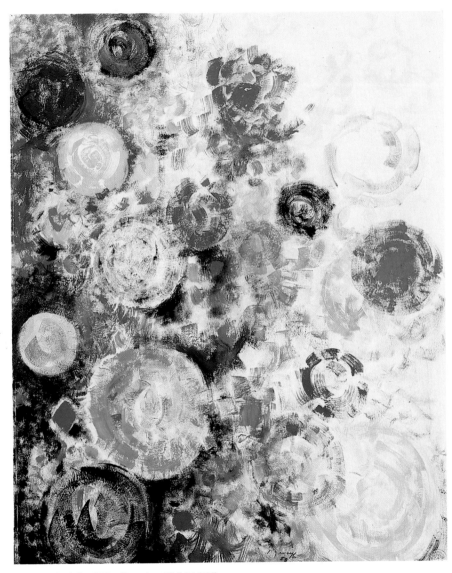

"Unititled," 1953, Casein, 23" X 29"

"Children's Corner," 1959, Oil, 34" X 39.5"

"Light of the Night," 1968-69, Oil, 48" X 34"

R.J.W. clockwise with Wendy, Elizabeth, and sons Pedro and Guy

R.J.W. in the studio with wife, Elizabeth

Dina in the barn sorting out the archival material, 1993

was that it coincided with the final evaporation of any interest I might ever have had in a college education.

In April of 1926, I simply stopped attending classes and for the next two months followed a way of life that was well suited to my own profane form of higher learning. I took long walks on those fragrant spring days, starting from my room in "Hush" Hall on the quadrangle, through the College Street gate to the New Haven Green, up stately Whitney Avenue to the Science buildings and then back again. I would sit on a bench or lie on the grass reading my renegade books, making notations on scraps of paper or just looking about me as haphazard thoughts and ideas ambled in and out of my consciousness.

It was on one of these days, while I was re-reading one of the short stories in Sherwood Anderson's *Winesburg, Ohio* called "The Book of the Grotesques," when I became aware that the old man in the story was trying to explain something which seemed to be identical to a passage I'd remembered from *The Brothers Karamazov*. When I returned to my room, I searched through the book until I found the quotation. I remember recording the following notation with a sense of elation at building a bridge between the insights of two of my literary heroes.

IRRECONCILABLES

Almost any line of thought that honestly endeavors to reach the substance of being will eventually be led to question its own validity simply because it has no final way of assuring itself of that validity. Any honest thinker will be self-conscious about this fact, and his sense of honesty will not let him alone until he states it.

Ivan in The Brothers Karamazov says, "I understand nothing. I don't want to understand anything now. I want to stick to the fact. I made up my mind long ago not to understand. If I try to understand anything I shall be false to the fact. And I have determined to stick to the fact."

The old man in Sherwood Anderson's **The Book of the Grotesques** has similar thoughts. "It was the truth that made the people grotesques. It was his notion that the moment one of the people took one of the truths to himself, called it his truth and tried to live by it, he became a grotesque and the truth he embraced became a falsehood."

🔲🔲🔲

ALTHOUGH I BADE FAREWELL to Yale shortly after this was written, I continued with my bridge building. Before the year was out, the notation begun

under the shade of an elm tree was completed in a rented room in Greenwich Village:

In different words Samuel Butler, in his **Note Books**, says somewhat
the same thing.

"We can neither define what we mean by truth nor be in doubt as
to our meaning. And this I suppose must be due to the antiquity of the
instinct that, on the whole, directs us towards truth. We cannot self-
vivisect ourselves in respect of such a vital function, though we can
discharge it normally and easily enough so long as we do not think
about it."

Henri Bergson puts it this way:

"Mechanism and finalism are therefore, here, only external views
of our conduct. They extract its intellectuality. But our conduct slips
between them . . . A conduct that is truly our own . . . is that of a will
which does not try to counterfeit intellect . . . The free act is incom-
mensurable with the idea . . . In explaining life by intellect (the conception of finality) limits too much the meaning of life."

Walt Whitman wrote a poem called, "When I Heard the Learn'd
Astronomer":

When I heard the learn'd astronomer,
When the proofs, the figures, were ranged in columns before me,
When I was shown the charts and diagrams, to add, divide and
measure them,
When I sitting heard the astronomer where he lectured with much
applause in the lecture-room,
How soon unaccountable I became tired and sick,
Till rising and gliding out I wander'd off by myself,
In the mystical moist night-air, and from time to time,
Look'd up in perfect silence at the stars[1].

Even more to the point is his poem, "A Song of the Rolling Earth":
The earth does not withhold, it is generous enough,
The truths of the earth continually wait, they are not so
conceal'd either,
They are calm, subtle, untransmissible by print,
They are imbued through all things conveying themselves
willingly,
Conveying a sentiment and invitation, I utter and utter,
I speak not, yet if you hear me not of what avail am I to you?

To bear, to better, lacking these of what avail am I to you?[2]

Anatole France in, I think it was **My Friend's Book**, says,

"Reason, proud reason, is capricious and cruel. The sacred simplicity of instinct never betrays. In instinct lies the sole truth, the only certitude that man may ever call his own in this world of illusion, where three-fourths of the ills we suffer proceed from our own thoughts."[3]

⊡ ⊡ ⊡

AS I SEE IT NOW, I could not have found a more appropriate lyric for my swan song to Yale.

Without revisiting any of my deserted classrooms, I presented myself to the notoriously gruff old fellow who was Dean of Students, Dean Jones to be sure, and with a burst of synthetic courage looked him in the eye and told him that I had had enough of Yale. The man, being used to dictating such leave taking, was somewhat dumbfounded when he discovered that my academic record, while far from brilliant, gave him no cause to happily confirm my decision. When he asked me, almost wistfully, why I was taking what seemed to him to be an insanely reckless course of action, I answered simply that Yale bored me. At that, his interest in my destiny suddenly evaporated, whereupon he shook my hand and wished me luck.

In the anteroom, his lady secretary who had overheard the proceedings, seemed quite pleased with me and gave me her hand in a gesture that was partially a farewell but seemed also to reflect approval, as though I were to be congratulated.

And so I walked out of the administration building under the delusion that I was leaving the scholastic life a free man with a free mind. In actuality, I was only leaping from the frying pan into the fire, that is to say from the gentle coercions of regimented learning to the more formidable coercions of industrial society where my precious free mind would be even more unwelcome than ever it was on Chapel Street.

[1] Whitman, Walt: "When I Heard the Learn'd Astronomer." The Norton Anthology of American Literature. 4th Ed. Vol 1. New York: W.W. Norton & Company, 1994. 2119.

[2] Whitman, Walt. Leaves of Grass. 1st Edition. New York: Viking Press, 1855.

[3] Anatole, France. My Friend's Book. Trans. J. Lewis May. New York: Park, Austin & Lipscomb, 1914.

PART IV

For reasons which will soon become clear I came directly to New York from New Haven and set about looking for a place to live on the edge of Greenwich Village in the vicinity of 13th Street and Fifth Avenue. I found a room to my liking in one of a row of old flat-fronted, balconied mansions on the south side of 10th Street halfway down the block, west of Fifth Avenue. The house was the last of many doorbells rung and stairs climbed and there was no doubt about the room the minute I saw it. It was on the fourth floor at the top of three very long flights of stairs. The sad-faced elderly lady who had answered the door led the way up. The first landing gave on a dark spacious living room with heavy furniture placed about in their white summer slipcovers flanked by well-polished tables of different sizes and shapes. Centered on the largest table was a Tiffany lamp with its glass shade of melancholy colors casting a pool of light on a plaster cast of a hand with its fingers limp and outstretched and looking very much at home in the somber, lifeless elegance that seemed to pervade the place.

When we reached the fourth floor, I was shown a large room with French doors giving on a narrow balcony of intricate iron grillwork which hung out over Tenth Street. What struck me most about the room was the bed. It was huge and rose high off the floor. Four tall posts carried a deeply valanced canopy which floated aloft like a celestial guardian. I moved myself and my few belongings into the room before the day was out and that night my sleep was long and deep.

Greenwich Village in 1926 was still a romantic bohemia peopled by artists and writers, cultural and political eccentrics and a happy hodgepodge of dissipated fugitives from all walks of Philistine respectability. Among the latter was my college friend and roommate, Edward Price Ehrich, whose precipitous exodus from Yale preceded mine by a year.

We had met for the first time at the dinner table the evening of my arrival at the Rosenbaum Tutoring School. There, we immediately discovered high-humored, irrepressible compatibility that kept us laughing and carousing together for the next two years, at the end of which Dean Jones abruptly separated us. Most uncharitably, Jones had decided that while Eddy had managed to pass each of his five courses, he had come so close to flunking them all that it amounted to the same thing. The just-passing grade was sixty, and Eddy had achieved what apparently no one in the memory of the Dean's office staff had ever done before him: he'd recorded a clean slate of five sixties on the nose. Eddy's older brother, a respected graduating senior, pleaded with the Dean, promising that he would see to it that the culprit would reform. But Jones scowled the words, "Wet Nurse" at him and that was that.

Ed Ehrich was no more at home on the Yale campus than was I, either socially or scholastically. More of a maverick than I, he took the whole matter of conventional education very lightly while I at least felt obliged, out of the far corners of my troubled conscience, to meet the monster half way. Although my efforts kept me on campus a bit longer, and while my departure was voluntary, we were both inevitably the discards of the same cultural syndrome. The only difference was that Ed's departure had a certain dramatic bang to it, while I just quietly dropped out, as they say today.

I was happy to rejoin him in New York, though we saw much less of each other than I had anticipated. We were both victims of the same disenchantment, both slightly disreputable exiles from organized respectability. But Eddy's rebellion was more open faced and thoroughgoing, and certainly more happy-go-lucky than mine. He shared an apartment deep in the West Village with a group of hard-drinking, fun-loving, kindred spirits: young journalists, actors, and writers who, like Ed, wanted to write novels. They took humdrum, work-a-day jobs against the day when somehow their, as yet undiscovered, talents would pay off. Of the group of five or six there are only two whose subsequent fate is now known to me. One was a tall, cheery fellow with a somewhat English accent named Archie Leach who eventually immigrated to California and became Cary Grant. The other was Ed himself, who after fourteen years and several self-shattering tries in the business world, wound up on a sandy point in Tahiti where he has remained ever since.

I have brought Ed Ehrich into this chronicle, first, because I've always had a great fondness for him, but more especially because he never seemed to be quite as trapped as I was by the ways and manners, the inane conventions and aspirations of mortal society which, as I now realize, is an earthbound version of the Shrinkers' side of Highbelovian life. While Ed was no paragon of Highbelovian virtues, his lighthearted rebellion against the accepted beliefs and behaviors of established respectability set an example for me in my confrontations with the same devil. Having have this moral (or amoral support, if you will) within walking distance was one of the reasons I chose the room on Tenth Street. The other reason was that I was to begin a kind of apprenticeship at an address on East 13th Street, just three short blocks away.

After having just said so firm a good-bye to Yale, I am forced to return there again to explain my presence in the summer of 1926 on the fifth floor of the rickety old building that housed the journalistic enterprises of the Fairchild Publications. And before Yale, I must turn back to Chicago, to a gentleman who presided over the fortunes of the clothing firm of Hart, Schaffner and Marx. Because of an old friendship with my parents, this man had become something of a foster uncle to me.

Uncle Al, as I shall call him, was a proudly self-made man with an enormous ego that quivered on the edge of his softly pitched voice, one that flirted with bursting through the seams of his stiff-backed, meticulously tailored dignity. Alexander M. Levy was a self-made, self-educated, self-inflated man whose rise from humble origins to the position of a man of wealth and worldly power was as much a source of snobbish pride as a Mayflower ancestor would be to a New England Brahmin. His wife Hana, Aunt Hana to me, was a brittle little woman with an overpowering willfulness which passed for adoring self-abnegation as she pampered and polished her hero's well-paid delusions of corporative and cultural grandeur.

They occupied an impressive apartment in the Drake Hotel, luxuriously furnished with their own antiquities, massive oriental rugs, heavy window drapes and tapestries, and a plethora of floor and table lamps hovering over deeply cushioned chairs and lounges. Most inescapable were the towering bookcases that covered the walls of one end of the living room from floor to ceiling. Here was where Uncle Al led his guests after a sumptuous dinner, sat them around him and then proceeded to spray them with undigested fragments of his extensive reading. Once he turned on the flow of self-intoxicating verbiage, there was nothing anyone could do to stop him. He was what might be described as intellectually short-winded. He could not follow through on any one subject without quickly running out of things to say about it. He must have prepared for an after dinner conversation the way a schoolboy anticipates an oral test on the homework he has done. There was no continuity to the tangled threads of his discourse that would wind its way through pronouncements praising Shakespeare just long enough to reel off a recently memorized couplet from King Lear, and then proceed to a perfect nonsequitur on the cunning ingenuities of Henry Thoreau's winter on Walden Pond. Trying to carry on a conversation with Uncle Al was like following the determined climb of a roller coaster up one steep incline after another where, each time after finally reaching the crest, you are allowed no time to take in the view before you're hurtled down to the start of another climb. I found Uncle Al's conversations and roller coasters equally nerve-wracking.

◙◙◙

(notation, November, 1946)

The key to vulgarity is not to be found in the vulgar act itself but in the motive behind it. Any act committed for its own sake cannot be vulgar. The same act committed for its effect would be. Behavior of the most delicate good taste could be thoroughly vulgar in design. If your satisfaction is in the act itself, whether it be a word, a dab of color, a thought, a belch, even a murder, you, at least, are no vulgarian.

◙◙◙

UNCLE AL AND AUNT HANA were childless. As a result, they turned to my sister and me as substitute objects of their frustrated parental instincts. They were genuinely fond of us and, in the way of parents, eager to influence the future course of our lives with the stuff that had shaped their own. I believe by the time I'd finished with Yale, Uncle Al had set his mind on a kind of self-perpetuating succession which, after a long period of careful grooming, would place me eventually in his shoes—socially, corporately, and financially. He and Aunt Hana did everything they could to make me into their crown prince. For a time I tried to fit into their scenario, but from the first, I knew in my heart that I had been miscast.

The intense pride Al Levy took in playing the part of a man of superior culture was not confined to the leisure hours of his private life. He carried his obsession with him wherever he went. He directed the affairs of a huge business enterprise devoted to the manufacture of men's clothing as though it were an institution with the highest cultural purposes. And while he was not unaware of mundane matters relating to profit and loss, I believe he left these commercial considerations to others while choosing to concentrate on a crusade to elevate the tone of the industry.

Uncle Al dressed himself in immaculately custom-tailored suits and was never without a white carnation in his lapel. He set an example of perfect grooming that made everyone around him look a bit shoddy. Actually his crusade had its practical aspects; he wanted to invest his mass produced ready-mades with the charisma of his own brand of ostentatious elegance. In the end, he actually had Hart, Schaffner and Marx looking down his nose at its customers, and not asking them, but telling them what style of clothing they should wear.

This is where I must return the reader once again to the Yale Campus. It was one day in early Fall of my junior year that a well dressed, middle-aged man knocked on my door and introduced himself as a friend of my uncle and an editor of a New York trade magazine covering the men's clothing industry. His mission was to commission me to write two articles each month relating to the latest apparel styles favored by Yale men. It must be remembered that Yale, at the time, was perhaps the most snob ridden center of learning in the east, with the possible exception of Groton Academy and Princeton University. On campus, there were hierarchies of social standing dominated by a clan of untouchables at the very top. What these paragons said, everyone repeated; where they went, everyone followed; and what they wore to cover their nakedness, everyone wore. My job was to be something in the nature of a private investigator, detecting any new oddities of apparel that the "best" people would periodically introduce by way of setting themselves apart.

It is true, as they used to say, that all Yale men dressed to look alike. Yet there were always innovators at the top of the ladder to break the sartorial monotony with a stylistic change of pace. Here was to be found the subject of my journalistic efforts. For the sum of $30 I was to write two articles a month to be called "Styles at Yale" for the edification of Hart, Schaffner and Marx and whoever among its competitors might wish to exploit the social inferiority of their youthful customers by persuading them to dress like Yale men.

I must confess, at this point, that I took a certain pride in my appearance and, in fact, spent much more time and money than I should have in haberdashery shops and tailoring establishments. The fact is, I never really got over my initial astonishment at finding myself a Yale man, and I suppose that dressing like one was a way of continually pinching myself to prove that it was true. However, if my interest in the vagaries of youthful fashions did nothing else, at least it helped me give the gentleman from the magazine exactly what he wanted. And although I did not let my success turn my head and, indeed, considered the whole project somewhat beneath me, I allowed myself a certain mild exhilaration at seeing my words in type for the first time. The articles were signed *R.J.W.*, which allowed me to hide my shame and serve my pride at one and the same time.

It seems I had no difficulty providing my readers with an endless stream of trivia on what the well dressed college man was currently wearing. One of my most impressive scoops involved fur coats. Part of the uniform which fashion prescribed for the typical Yale man was the raccoon coat. Everyone on campus who could afford one wore one. It so happened on one bitter cold winter morning when I was hurrying across the quadrangle that I caught sight of one of the untouchables (Captain of the Polo Team, Skull and Bones, DKE, Boston Brahmin, etc.) striding down the walk in my direction. He was a giant of a lad and, with a senior's privilege, was hatless. But, to my astonishment, in place of the expected raccoon he was covered from his ears to his ankles in black bear skin. This was an innovation so utterly out of place that only one of the better of the best people would have dared to wear it. As the bear skin passed with a nod of its head I turned in my tracks and returned to my room where I dashed off an article predicting the replacement of the raccoon by the black bear in the hearts of rich, young college men.

The article caused quite a stir in the New York editorial offices and my editor made a special trip to New Haven to make certain that the facts were as I had stated them. The article was published without change and, while not another black bear coat appeared on the Yale Campus all winter, my article was enough to start a vogue that quickly spread throughout the hinterland of this country. This absurdly far-reaching consequence of a few silly words printed on a page gave me something new to think about.

It appears that my articles convinced Al Levy that his confidence in me was not misplaced for, by the time I decided to quit Yale, he had made rather elaborate plans for my immediate future. Through his friends and connections at the Fairchild Publications, he arranged a kind of apprenticeship, first in their office of textile design research, and then as a cub reporter on their daily newspaper, covering the menswear industry. These arrangements were to terminate at the end of six months and I was then to join the firm of Hart, Schaffner and Marx for a year of sartorial and cultural polishing in the office of their London representative. The immediate prospect of a pleasant summer in New York, followed by a year abroad, overcame any misgivings I might have had about making the manufacture of men's clothing my life's work.

One of the greatest strokes of sheer good fortune that has ever come to me was my first assignment at the Fairchild Publications. I had already had a long, rambling letter from one M.D.C. Crawford explaining that he had agreed to take me under his wing for a short time.

Mr. Robert J. Wolff
Sisson Hotel
Fifty-third St. A The Lake
Chicago, Illinois
Dear Mr. Wolff:

I received one telegram from Mr. Levy and one from yourself, and can only say that I will be delighted to see you at your own convenience. I have thought very much both of the responsibility and the opportunity you offer me.

For many years it has been my deep conviction that all industry administering to the aesthetic values, such as personal adornment and the decoration of domiciles, has sadly felt the need of a fundamental understanding of the history of the emotions and reactions developed through form, texture and color.

I cannot believe it is possible to intellectualize to safe conclusions. Experiments in materials and their use are essential. The introduction of the machine has placed a social premium on training and mental aptitude capable of organized machinery, and particularly on the disposing of the ever-increasing bulk of machine production. As machine technique tends to stabilization, the engineer gives place to the salesman. This is particularly true in the great bulk of fabric production. The mill man responsible for the management of labor and the running of the machines is completely dominated by the trader. Standards, styles, qualities, etc. are determined not by the capacity of the machine nor by the actual social needs of the community, but by the judgment of this individual as factors effect salability. If we eliminate, therefore, the equation of profit, the direction of the system will often resemble the maundering of idiots.

I do not wish to express any opinion on economic philosophy. . . . You cannot cure or destroy the world with a form of words. But in order to get the facts, or rather the philosophy, of the decorative arts, we must eliminate from our consideration any superstitious reverence for the status quo of modern economic society. Because I am contented and rather indolent, I sincerely hope that I shall always be engaged in a business that yields a profit. I trust your own ventures will be equally, if not more profitable, than mine. . . .

It is desirable, therefore, in my belief, that you first address your-self to a study of the philosophy of primitive material culture. The basis of all modern industry is obviously the craft arts of primitive people—pottery, basket making, wood and stone carving, the making of ornaments and the great textile arts. Here certainly lie the basic ideas that will direct machine production. Your method of approach to these subjects should express rather your own individuality than any par-ticular form or code of study. Your interest will be slightly at variance with my own and with any other man's, and I tell you frankly, it makes no difference how you approach the problem, so long as the ap-proach lies along paths constantly pleasant to yourself. No matter what your own force of character or self-control may be, in the long run you will retain only the things that you want and to encumber yourself with the methods of others will muddle the clarity and lucid-ity of your internal vision upon which all external expression ulti-mately depends. . . .

I have certainly no wish that you should take an academic posi-tion in regard to the useful and interesting work before you. Men dis-like to be educated and the less your associates know of the training you are giving yourself, the happier everybody will be. Personally, I make a strong effort to treat lightly the processes by which I have ar-rived at certain conclusions.

I have no doubt that your method of approach, and even certain of your conclusions, will be at variance with my own. I hope so. I have all the defects and limitations of a pioneer, and of course, you can see my mistakes and limitations much more clearly than I can myself. I will very gladly, however, open to you as far as possible the same sources of inspiration that were open to me and gladly confer with you as your work develops.

I warn you, there are no formulae. There is no specific course of in-struction. It will not be easy and I can only promise you as a reward the association with objects of beauty and interest and a clear understand-ing of the relationship that craftsmanship bears to machine production.

You have been invited by Mr. Edward L. Mayer to attend his opening on the 21st. of June. You can either come then or earlier suiting your own convenience and I will give you as much time as I can possibly spare from my work. . . . Cordially yours . . .

◫◫◫

Morris Crawford was then in his middle forties. He was a big man with big hands and an enormous head. He was explosively articulate, totally extroverted and, astonishingly, at the same time, a sensitive man of genius. He and his staff, consisting of three young artists and a secretary, occupied several rooms on the top floor of the old building, one of which served as his private office, library, workroom, and general meeting place. Here, he held court and received all comers with unflagging high spirits. His conversation ranged erratically from baseball lore to the art of Eskimos and his language was so colorful that its effect on people was almost hypnotic. Here he gave over his inexhaustible energies to the quixotic crusade to raise the aesthetic standards of the American textile industry by trying to persuade it to give mind to man's vast cultural heritage.

M.D.C. Crawford was perhaps one of the first Americans to confront the vulgarities of mass production with the exquisite standards of ancient traditions. He proposed that technology provide itself with human eyes and so give some thought to art. I listened open-mouthed and tongue-tied as the man unburdened his mind in non-stop soliloquies that could be heard by anyone within shouting distance.

I never quite understood the exact nature of Crawford's value to the Fairchild Publications. I believe he was retained as a consultant by companies involved in various facets of textile design and manufacture. It is my guess that it was as much his personal magnetism as his practical usefulness that got him the job. He was, for one thing, a professional ethnologist, well known for his scholarship in the art of primitive and archaic cultures and particularly for his work on the art of Pre-Incan Peru. He gave me several of his scholarly publications to read, one of which was a fascinating pamphlet published by the Museum of Natural History. Here, the weaving techniques of the ancient Peruvians was revealed through a painstaking analysis of surviving fragments of their exquisite cotton tapestries, which Crawford insisted were the finest ever woven, not excepting the Coptic masterpieces of the Early Christian Era in Egypt. He managed somehow to make a count, per-inch, of the fibers under a microscope and arrived at a number between two- and three-hundred.

If the reader will recall certain characteristics of the spiritually robust Expander workman of Highbelow, he will find overtones of the same endowments in this remarkable man. Crawford, from the first moment I set eyes on him in his office/workroom, seemed to me a man from another world, alien to his industrial surroundings even though he was obviously and noisily in command of them. His office shelves and walls were filled with ancient objects and artifacts from Mexico, North and South America, and the Polynesian cultures of the South Pacific. There were wood and stone sculptures, pottery, jewelry, and printed fabrics of all kinds. When he expressed his love of these things, he spoke little about the intangibles of their sheer beauty, focusing instead on the marvelously disciplined craftsmanship, the inherent originality and inventiveness that never violated ancient traditions but rather somehow subtly enriched and extended them. Crawford revealed to me the essence of perfect taste in visual matters without ever mentioning the phrase or defining the condition. It was a quality of being unequivocally and inevitably right. Many years later, in making the following notation, I was simply recording a facet of knowledge that M.D.C. Crawford had given me, not by word of mouth, but by an act of the eye:

(notation, 1951)

What is good taste? You find it in things that men make about which it can be said that this was necessarily so.

🔳🔳🔳

My favorite quotation from Samuel Butler appealed to me originally, I am sure, as a result of the effect of Crawford's outlook on my own way of seeing things.

(notation, 1950)

"It must be remembered that no work is required to be more than right as far as it goes; the greatest cannot get beyond this and the least comes strangely near the greatest if this can be said of it."

🔳🔳🔳

THE FORMAL COURSE OF STUDY in the history of art of which I partook at Yale was a lifeless affair compared to the eye-opening form of learning that I casually experienced under Morris Crawford. In New Haven, there was something quite inert about the dull photographic images projected on the screen or the lecture hall or filed away page after page in a loose leaf notebook. And the voice which day after day intoned its remote scholarly pronouncements was a poor thing compared to the explosive, slightly profane vernacular with which M.D.C. would project an affinity with the products of men's hands and eyes. For the first time in my life, works of art no longer remained dead, but highly prized documents of recorded history. They had become as alive as the human beings who had fashioned them. I began to forge a new link between the past and the present, between the dead and the living, to feel, in one, the essence of the other, until they merged into an ever present oneness. An intricately carved wooden canoe paddle made long ago by a native of New Guinea, displayed now in a case at the museum of Natural History, gave my eyes a new kind of beauty to absorb and understand, but it also gave me an exhilarating sense of the wholeness of time where lost hours, days, and years were miraculously recovered and incarnated into carved images. My teacher never tried to teach me anything. He wisely confronted me with a world where learning was simply an inescapable facet of open-eyed wakefulness.

◧ ◧ ◧

THE FOLLOWING IS AN EXCERPT FROM A WOLFF LECTURE GIVEN AT THE BARLOW SCHOOL, APRIL 1966, PUBLISHED IN MANAS, 1972:

One day, several years ago, when I was pondering the difficulties involved in attempting to open doorways to art, I turned the clock back on my own student days when life was a succession of new and wondrous revelations and where, one after the other, new doorways to art were magically swinging open.

I hoped that if I could rediscover how it all happened to me, I might find clues that would help others. I recalled the years I spent in Paris as a student of sculpture. My mornings were spent at the *Ecole des Beaux Arts,* and later at the *Academie Julien.* Every afternoon, I would cross to the right bank of the Seine and head for the Louvre. I would hurry through the long corridors housing the master paintings of Western art to stairs that led me to my destination—the far corner of the basement where the stone carvings of Archaic Greece were placed. My obsessive love for these austere monuments blinded me to everything else. For many months, day after day, I would pass masterpieces by Rubens, Claude de Lorraine, Chardin, and all the others with merely a glance here and there as I made my way to my basement paradise. This went on for some time, until one day when I stopped in front of a still life by the 18th Century painter Chardin and found to my astonishment that it suddenly came to life for me.

100

As time went on, my dash through the corridors slowed to an ambling walk and one by one I discovered the miracles of the painter's art that had, until then, been obscured by impatience, unfamiliarity, and indifference. I have never lost the magic of these first revelatory experiences, and I am sure the deep impact that was made was prepared by the many months of casual exposure that my daily journeys to the basement provided. Had I been stopped in my tracks as I hurried by these works and been forced by some earnest docent to shed my indifference to Rubens through expert elucidation before I was ready, I know the doorway to this master would have remained closed to me for many more years, if not forever.

Remembering how the life in these masterworks was revealed to me by reason of sheer and prolonged exposure and contact, not long ago when I was wondering what to do about the indifference of many art students to the great works of the past, it occurred to me that they may be actually relying on educational concepts to replace personal insight—that they may in fact know too much about things to which they have never, in reality, been exposed. I thought that if I could simulate the conditions of my youthful experience in the Louvre, I might hope for similar results. However, I could hardly force students to take a daily walk in Central or Prospect Park, following a path that would lead through one door of either the Brooklyn or Metropolitan museums and out the other end. The best solution that came to mind was a plan to require all Art majors to spend one full day a week in one of our major art museums. They would be clocked in at nine in the morning and clocked out at four in the afternoon. There would be no instruction, no guided tours. They would be on their own, free to spend their time as they pleased, as long as they stayed on the premises. They could even sleep if they could find some suitable corner for the purpose. The one objective would be, not to teach them about art, but to put them in direct contact with works of art and to force on them a prolonged exposure. For this, they would receive two credits towards the Baccalaureate degree with no questions asked.

For a while, I played with the idea of proposing this plan for academic approval. I still may someday, when higher education gets around to giving as much thought to the conditions under which knowledge is absorbed as it does to knowledge alone.

◻◻◻

Aᴠᴛᴇʀ ꜱᴏᴍᴇ ᴡᴇᴇᴋꜱ, I began to spend more and more time in museums among the collections of primitive and archaic art and in thumbing through illustrated books in museum libraries. I filled my notebooks not with dates and names and places, but with crude drawings of crafted things and objects that especially delighted me. Crawford was never too busy to stop what he was doing to answer my questions and examine my drawings. He seemed to find enjoyment in my growing involvement in his world of art and responded to my innocent enthusiasms with long and fascinating discourses, sometimes to the neglect of pressing office work. Often, he would be interrupted in the midst of one of these monologues by his ever-worried secretary who would try desperately to attract his attention in the interest of the many urgent practical matters that he habitually neglected. To get through to him at moments like this was, no doubt, one of the most harassing of the poor lady's many jobs.

These were happy and rewarding days, filled with the excitement of my new freedom and the discovery of an unknown self. This was the summer of 1926 and I was about to reach my twenty-first birthday. Looking back, my life seems to have been a continuous exertion of will to discover certain lost identities that, once revealed, appeared to have always been at hand, needing only an open eye and receptive mind to again become intimate realities. There was something shockingly unexpected in the suddenly discovered loveliness of a tapa cloth from the Fiji Islands—unexpected and at the same time strangely familiar, as though what I saw was known, but just recently remembered. It seemed to me that I was reaching back in time to a lost existence that had no place in the present and was attainable only in scattered fragments. Morris Crawford came into my life, perhaps, to reawaken and revive my benumbed Highbelovian sensibilities and to strengthen the will to return to the life I had once known in Highbelow.

This delightful period away from the practical demands of the business world, which I would inevitably have to face, came to an end sooner than I would have wished. Somehow, after three months, it was decided, no doubt at the behest of my good uncle, that it was time to terminate the purely artistic side of my indoctrination and to introduce me to the brass knuckles of business enterprise. Although I was sorry to leave Morris Crawford's private world of art, I accepted my new assignment with a nervous eagerness that tried, but never succeeded to overcome my deep misgivings.

The gruff aggressiveness of Crawford's extroverted personality did not always hide his sensitivity that occasionally bordered on the sentimental. I believe he was fully aware that I was, by nature, unsuited for the plunge I was about to take. For a week before my scheduled transfer to the city desk of the firm's daily newspaper, he lectured me on the need to toughen up, that life was not going to be quite the same on the second floor as it had been on the fifth. He was, in fact, even more worried about my inadequacies than I was, and he cautioned and encouraged me with the concern of a mother sending her little boy into the rough and tumble of the schoolyard for the first time. I think he worried that I had become more involved in the impractical delights of art than he had intended and felt obliged to explain that art has never been an easy way of life, and that gifted people have always had to make compromises in coming to terms with the work-a-day world. And then he would tell me how John Masefield had written some of his best poetry while working as a bartender in a Bowery saloon, and how Rousseau the painter made his living as a customs official. He seemed to be trying to warn me that I was going to have one hell of a time being myself, and at the same time, the future president of Hart, Schaffner and Marx.

Finally, the morning came when I followed him into the rickety old elevator that took us down to the second floor where he turned me over to a tight-faced individual sitting behind an untidy desk. I felt very small as M.D.C. left me standing there while he moved through the crowded room toward the elevator, admonishing the city editor in a loud voice to ignore my inexperience and put me to work on the roughest assignments he could find. I smiled appreciatively at Crawford's joke as he walked away and turned to my new boss to share my amusement. He was not laughing.

For some reason, I cannot remember much about the man save that he was grim faced and spoke little about anything but the business at hand. I was assigned to a small desk with an ancient typewriter and was told what was expected of me in the fewest possible words. There was an accumulation of insignificant and unpleasant reportorial assignments that no one on the regular staff could be persuaded to accept and which were held in abeyance for the day when someone as innocent and dispensable as myself would arrive on the scene. The list that was given me asked for interviews with traveling representatives of clothing and textile firms, descriptions of the renovated interiors of certain retail clothing establishments, reports on the views of certain sales managers regarding business conditions, and so on. I distinctly remember a disturbing dryness of the mouth and a feeling of general numbness, combined with the perspiring discomfort of a badly ventilated room as I contemplated the kind of work that confronted me. The job of bartender in a Bowery saloon seemed lovely by comparison.

When Mr. Hadley, as I shall call my boss, handed me the list, he underlined one item in red ink, indicating that I was to attend to it first and to lose no time about it. The item in question referred to the name (which I've forgotten) of a cotton mill executive from Houston, Texas with a New York address, followed by the word, "interview." The address was a room number in the Biltmore Hotel, and when I asked Hadley in all good faith what the interview was to be about, he said he was damned if he knew and advised me to find out from the man himself. I also had the temerity to ask the reason for the urgency of the interview and was answered by a blank look as he picked up his telephone and began talking into it.

It did not take me long to find out that none of the instructional niceties provided by the fifth floor could be expected on the second, where no one had the slightest interest in the educational aspects of my presence there and where, from the first, I was all but ignored as an unwelcome encumbrance. I felt very much alone and somewhat frightened. Indeed it was cold, perspiring fright that I felt as I sat in the back seat of a Fifth Avenue bus as it carried me uptown to the Biltmore Hotel. During that dismal journey of thirty short crosstown blocks, I suffered through a soul shattering blue funk. As the bus maneuvered its way slowly through the congested traffic, I scrawled suggestions and reminders in a little notebook and then immediately crossed them out to replace them with new ideas that would, in turn, be swiftly discarded. By the time we crossed 42nd Street, I was in a panic of anxiety. I stumbled off the bus and headed for the reception desk of the Biltmore Hotel. I waited numbly as the room clerk telephoned to announce my presence. Then, as I turned and walked toward the elevators, I realized (as in a dream) that I had absolutely nothing to say to the gentleman who was waiting to receive me.

(notation, circa 1955)

I am a very brave man.
I have to be.
I am easily frightened.

🔲🔲🔲

I HAVE FORGOTTEN HOW the interview began, but I suppose I had the wit to introduce myself and mumble through whatever amenities I could think of to avoid falling into the conversational vacuum that threatened me like Doomsday. I do not know what I said or whether or not it made much sense but the words came fast and fluently, as though someone had wound me up then suddenly unsprung me. I do not remember much about the man, except that he was middle-aged, thick set and bald, and he wore gaudy suspenders over a stiffly starched white shirt. I especially remember the suspenders. For my eyes fastened upon them in my eagerness to avoid the tongue-tying effects of looking him straight in the face. The man was distressingly taciturn, saying so little that a brief pause from me would become an insane silence into which I would again have to plunge with whatever I could find on the tip of my tongue. It was plain that the fellow was letting me know that it was he, not I, who was to be interviewed and that he had no intention of encouraging or comforting me as I proceeded with the business at hand in an agony of ineptitude.

I remember sitting stiffly in a straight-backed chair at a flat desk while my friend stretched out in a deeply upholstered armchair and stared at me with a sleepy serenity that I found utterly unnerving. I remember plying him with frantically improvised questions on his impressions of New York, the length of his stay, the purpose of his visit, and the nature of his business, to which he responded briefly and almost absent-mindedly. As I sat there perspiring and recording the inane information in my notebook, it seemed to me that the ordeal would never end. Finally, I asked a question that inadvertently closed the interview. What it was I cannot recall, but its effect was to induce the verbal impasse that I had been trying to avoid for the past half-hour. For some reason, the man stubbornly refused to give me an answer. I remember repeating the question after a long silence. My second attempt to get an answer, any answer, just to break the stillness, was as futile as the first. He just sat there and stared blankly at me. And I, for my part, with a stubbornness born of desperation, sat equally silent with my pencil poised expectantly as I stared with glazed eyes at my notebook. This time, I was damned, come what may, if I would not have the last word.

After what seemed an interminable silence, the man rose from his chair with a smile and congratulated me for having conducted an excellent interview, and then proceeded to ask if I would like to work for him in Houston, Texas. I somehow politely declined the offer, tucked my notebook away, and bade him good-bye. Walking down the hotel corridor I had to shake my head violently like a wet dog to prove that I was alive and sane.

The next day in one of the back pages of the *Daily News Record* there appeared a short paragraph near the bottom announcing the arrival in New York from Houston, Texas, of Mr. So-and-So of such-and-such a company on a buying mission. When I saw the absurd thing, I have to admit that I was shamelessly proud of it.

During the next few weeks, I learned much about the intricacies and hazards of the Metropolitan subway system as I traveled from one trivial assignment to the next, from the opening of a Madison Avenue haberdashery shop to a warehouse fire sale in Brooklyn. I covered enormous distances, mostly in hot, crowded subway cars, but sometimes by bus or streetcar. At the end of the day I would return to my desk with a sheaf of notes and type out little insipid "stories" containing the details of all the dull information I had gathered. After dropping these in the outgoing basket for the next day's editions I would drag myself out of the place, depressed by the thought of having given so much and accomplished so little. The fact was, however, I was doing well at the silly job. There were no complaints or criticisms and my inane little paragraphs always appeared without alteration. The saving factor was my writer's vanity. Although I despised what I wrote, I would return to my desk each morning and eagerly search the morning edition for my contributions. Seeing the awful stuff in print seemed to purify it somehow.

My life after working hours, although quiet and uneventful, was pleasant enough. There were numbers of small restaurants and speakeasies tucked away in the basements of the old buildings that lined the narrow streets of Greenwich Village where I would enjoy excellent, inexpensive food and drink alone, or occasionally with friends. It was at this time that I made the happy discovery that I was never bored with my own company and that I very much liked going about by myself. I took particular pleasure in the open-air symphony concerts that, in recent years, had been inaugurated at Lewisohn Stadium, an hour's bus ride far up into the Bronx. I would board the empty bus at Eighth Street, take a front seat on the open upper deck, and let myself be carried up Fifth Avenue through the twilight of the early evening. As I looked around me and upward through the canyons of tall buildings, my spirits would soar, my eyes would absorb the passing scene, and my mind would open to a multitude of migrant thoughts.

I believe it was on these bus trips that I first became aware of the mutually exclusive relationship of active thought and active vision. I discovered that thinking and seeing were two different kinds of awareness and that concentrated thinking blinded the seeing eye just as undistracted visual concentration turned off the thinking mind.

I remember one evening as I looked around me from the top of the bus, my attention became suddenly riveted on the large, blocked-out letters that spelled the name of a business firm over the entrance to a building where the bus had stopped. The name I have forgotten, but the word COMPANY tacked on the end of it suddenly became grotesquely unfamiliar.

For an instant or two I had the frightening sense of having lost my mind. For the word suddenly meant nothing to me. I suppose I had become so mind-lessly alive in a visual sense that I saw the word COMPANY merely as an object and had turned off the mental machinery that would read a meaning into it. The experience must have impressed me deeply, for I have never forgotten it; and the next time I was similarly confronted, I recorded the fol-lowing notation:

(New York, 1926)

Every now and then I am visited by the most appalling blankness of mind which curiously can lead again to startlingly lucid revelation. It must be that to regain fresh and original perception, one must com-pletely purge oneself of habitual manners of mind, of reflex knowledge. One finds oneself staring chaos in the face. It is confusing and frighten-ing until one reflects upon it. And then, somehow, one finds that the experience has been good.

For example, I begin a letter. I write, "Dear friends." I look at the word "friends" and it suddenly seems that I have never seen it before, that it belongs to some strange, unknown language. I stare at it and try to regain the easy familiarity with which I unconsciously spelled it out. The more I stare, the more like gibberish it seems. I reverse the spelling of the "ie," thinking that perhaps the letter arrangement is wrong. The situation becomes more chaotic. Something like a feeling of panic comes over me.

Words, instead of unconsidered vehicles of thought, suddenly be-come monstrous hieroglyphics, related to nothing, terrible in their meaninglessness. There they are, great grotesques over which I have lost control, and which have turned against me. I am in the dilemma of the sorcerer's apprentice. I am the victim of my own careless belief in my skill with the magic of language. The mysterious knowledge that I arrogantly took for granted deserts me and I find myself face to face with the word "friends," ignorant as the day I was born. How and when and whether I shall regain the key to the mystery is not impor-tant. I shall, of course. On the other hand, such contact with chaos can be momentous, and reflection upon it purifying.

◫ ◫ ◫

AND SO BEGAN what has been a lifelong war of the words and the marks, a standoff battle between writing and painting, an incurable dichotomy between thought and sight. Some forty years after the above notation was made I followed through with this:

(circa, 1966)
THE WAR OF WORDS AND MARKS
A STATEMENT BY ONE OF ITS VICTIMS

There is one thing that most artists have in common, that being a final indifference to the interpretive concept, to truth without consequences, to the word without music, to thought without action. Because of this resistance to word-thoughts, they do not write, or if they do, they tend to write exasperated nonsense.

I have always had a stubborn and unreasonable fear of words, I mean my own words. By the time each one untangles itself from the semantic jungle and is tested to make sure its meaning fits the nameless reality that claimed it, the whole action of experience is slowed down to the point where the continuity of time and fact is destroyed, and the real truth leaves me behind with an empty but dogged preoccupation with a word puzzle. When I write, my feelings must be somewhat like the runner who has to stop in the middle of a race to tie his shoelace.

I have never had this sense of frustrated inaction while painting, even when confronted with difficult craft problems. The easy answer to this, of course, is that I am by nature a painter and not a writer. But the fact that I may be more at ease with paint than with words does not explain away the fact that painting is cause and consequence in itself, and as an act it is whole, tangible and self-evident. A word, no matter how exquisitely appealing to the senses, is an action whose consequences must be deduced before its reality is complete. When I read or write there is always the sense that life is circling about me and that I stand in a vacuum struggling with an abstraction.

On the contrary, when I paint or listen to music, I have a heightened sense of implicit aliveness, a condition that surely is instinctively the goal of all living things.

To me, the word is like a vortex into which reality rushes and is consumed. In recreating its captive in its own image, it instills it with the vitality it has drained from the act of life. And when the job is done, you look up from the weirdly alive illusion to discover that it has been feeding on a corpse.

Unlike the word, the mark is not a parasite. It is a force in itself like all other living things. One can make a mark without dying a bit. One can leave a painting and find reality untouched, intact and alive.

Then why do I write? I suppose, like many thoughtful human beings, I cannot let well enough alone and allow the action of life to speak for itself. My resistance to qualifying, explaining and describing has been great, but not great enough. I resent being pulled into the vacuum of recorded knowledge, but my thoughts, whatever they are, have the weakness of vanity and would rather trade the certainty of anonymous truth for a precarious identity.

As I write these words, my paintings withdraw and watch me from a distance like strangers.

◨◨◨

notation, June 27, 1971:

I love my paintings because they give me nothing to think about.

◨◨◨

DURING THE WEEKS THAT FOLLOWED, I endured the depressing monotony of my daily tasks and doggedly made the rounds of news sources for my little stories. For some reason that must have to due to my faltering self-esteem, I carefully cut every insignificant printed paragraph and filed the clips in a special box in my desk. One evening as I was leaving the building, I was more than usually depressed by the effects of the day's work and was, in fact, angered at the prospect of going on with the same exasperating routine day after day. My resentment, for want of any other victim, centered on my boss, the city editor. I began to hate the matter-of-fact way he would hand over my list of ridiculous assignments each morning without even looking at me and then go on with what he was doing as though I did not exist. I began to wonder what I could do to break through his insulting indifference and make him take some notice of me.

After dinner that evening, I started walking aimlessly up lower Fifth Avenue when it occurred to me a visit to the Public Library would be time well spent if I could find something more interesting to write about men's clothes than the usual inanities that were expected of me. I had no idea what I would find, but I decided then and there to board a bus and spend the evening in the big building on 42nd Street.

For an hour or so, I thumbed through a stack of books on the history of men's fashions and finally settled on a little book published in England on the evolution of styles in men's hats. After reading a while, I came upon a story that I recognized at once for the very thing I had come to find. It described how, early in the 19th Century, a certain gentleman of fashion had his hatmaker build a tall head covering of shiny black silk that would sit on his head like a stovepipe. When the splendid thing was ready he popped it on his head, left the hat shop, and made his way down the center of Bond Street. The effect on passersby in the crowded thoroughfare was so infuriating that fights broke out and the riot that ensued finally had to be quelled by the police, who found it necessary to lock up many of the embattled participants. And this, I wrote as I brought the story to a close, was the way the first silk top hat made its appearance among men.

The next morning, Mr. Hadley found me waiting for him as he settled down at his desk. He sifted through some papers in a basket, extracted three or four and handed them to me. I took them and, as usual, he ignored me and turned to other matters on his desk. He soon became aware that I had remained standing there, and he looked up at me with a startled frown on his face. He said nothing and I waited. I handed him my silk hat story, saying I had been doing some evening research at the public library and had happened upon a story that he might want to use. I left the typed page on his desk and walked away without a word from him.

The story appeared in a neat little box on the front page of the next day's morning edition. I was so overjoyed at the sight of it that I recklessly approached the city desk for a word or two of praise from Mr. Hadley. He was waiting for me as I approached and asked me outright how in hell I could have found that story at the public library when it had been cabled in during the night from the London office.

"The exact same story?" I asked incredulously.

"Yes," he said, "the same damn story in different words."

I protested that the odds against such a thing happening were unthinkable. He agreed, but assured me that there was no doubt about the coincidence.

I walked back to my desk in a daze. I did not complete my assignments that day because I could not keep my mind on them. And the really funny thing about the episode was that Mr. Hadley treated me like any other human being from that day on.

The story of the silk hat made the rounds of the building. The other editor, whom I had known at Yale, must have suddenly been reminded of my presence on the second floor. For one day I was asked to join him at Mr. Hadley's desk for a short conference. Here, it was decided that for the next few days I would confine my news gathering to the uptown area centering on the stores and shops of Madison Avenue where the well-to-do men of New York clothed themselves. I was to report on what the well dressed man was wearing. Although I did not relish the prospect of renewing the nonsense of men's fashions that I had left behind at Yale, it was, for the moment, a welcome change from what I had been doing. About this time, I confided to Morris Crawford at lunch one day that I was depressed by the waste of effort in writing so much about so little, whereupon he told me to cheer up because at my age whatever I wrote about would result in empty verbiage, so it might as well be about shirts and pants. He told me I needed practice in word making and to do my prose scales on my typewriter on the second floor. He also told me to stop complaining. Needless to say, I resented his good advice.

I made a success of my new assignment if, for no other reason, that it exploited my weakness for elegantly well-made wearing apparel. I wasted hours standing in front of display windows and examining the merchandise in stores up and down Madison and Fifth Avenues. I was soon told to combine my reports into a daily column which I called "North of 42nd Street" simply because nothing fashionable seemed to happen south of 42nd Street. Before long, I found that I could go about my business without anyone's interference. The work was easy and innocuous and seemed to be what everyone wanted. I was quite content with my new status, but before my highly successful daily column was many weeks old, Mr. Al Levy arrived in town to announce the end of my newspaper apprenticeship and the start of a career with Hart, Schaffner and Marx. The plan was to send me to England for a year under the aegis of the firm's London office and I was to start at once. I readily agreed.

However, before I bid good-bye to my friends on 13th Street, I had the pleasure of witnessing an attempted high level double-cross when I was called into the executive offices of the newspaper and offered a whopping fifty dollars a week to desert Hart, Schaffner and Marx. Politely refusing the offer gave me a certain pleasure and a quite irrational sense of my own importance.

(notation, June 26, 1971, Wellfleet)

In the late spring of 1926 I came to New York City disillusioned
and bored with college life, and settled into an exciting but bewildering

new life. What struck me hardest was the frightening impersonality of the city man whose individuality was abstracted into the massive collective identity of **men** as a conceivable, tangible thing. I worried this thought into a poem which I think I called **Manhattan** (written in 1928 in New York upon my return from England). It was addressed to a city dweller, cautioning him to come down from his perch high in his sky-scraping home to the street below, because looking down from forty stories he could see only crowds of men, never an individual man. I pleaded with him to forget **men** because there was no such thing, **men** being a convenient delusion relieving him of the necessity to face the reality of the **man** himself.

Finally, I suggested that our language should be changed, throwing out the word **men** as the plural of man—and that, when more than one man is spoken of, the word should be **mans**. **Mans** does not inflate humanity into a massive abstraction but maintains the presence of the individual within the multiple concept.

◧◧◧

WRITING OUT OF ONE'S PAST has its hazards. How does one explain why an impression from early childhood may remain vividly clear while a recent experience may dissolve and disappear as though it never happened? As I retrace the passage of time and reach back into the past, I can find only what my memory chooses to give back. Much that I would like to relive escapes me, leaving only bits and pieces that may partially recall the lost reality but can never fully restore it.

There was, for example, the crossing of the Atlantic through the late December storms of 1926 on the liner, *Majestic*. The only thing that I remember with any clarity is the weather. I had made the crossing many times before but not in the winter. I had never been troubled by seasickness and I survived this trip without it, although I believe I was one of the few passengers who did. On the second day out, the huge ship began to roll, pitch, and plunge. At one point it seemed determined to capsize. I remember being seated in an arm chair on one side of the main saloon when the ship started a slow roll in the opposite direction, lifting me higher and higher untill I found myself on a hilltop from which I slid off my chair and continued across the room on my backside until I crashed into a steward trying to carry a tray. I came to a stop at the opposite side of the room and waited breathlessly while the ship decided against going over all the way and began slowly to right herself.

The storm continued unabated for most of the trip and I was glad to finally disembark at Plymouth and board the London-bound train. I settled into the corner of an empty second class compartment where, for the next few hours, I slowly recovered my sense of well being as I contemplated the passing countryside and the uncertain future that awaited me. There was only one thing that really troubled me: I did not see how I would be able to endure my new boss.

Captain Jack Murdock was a total phony. It was as though some evil genius with a perverse sense of humor had collected a bag full of the oddest human characteristics he could find and manufactured a man from them. I had had my first unbelieving glimpse of him one day, coming out of one of the Fairchild executive offices, then met him face to face at a small dinner party arranged by Aunt Hana and Uncle Al on one of their New York visits.

Captain Murdock was the London representative of Hart, Schaffner and Marx and a writer for the Fairchild Publications. He claimed to be the world's best dressed man and the highest authority on men's fashions in the English speaking world. His employers indulged him in this fantasy as a matter of business policy. For his style pronouncements made news for the one and stimulated the sale of clothing for the other. They treated him with the greatest deference, like commoners deferring to a reigning prince. Jack Murdock's title of "Captain" was fictitious, like everything about him. It is possible that even the name itself was a fabrication. There was something too dashingly appropriate about it to be true.

He was waiting for me on the station platform in all his well dressed glory. He was a slight man whose clothes were so formidably constructed that his body seemed not to belong to his face, the impression being something like an undernourished knight in shining armor looking through the open visor of his headpiece. There was nothing about this man that was believable. He was totally and impeccably artificial.

After an exchange of greetings, the Captain suddenly became *Mister* Murdock. No time was lost to admonish me against calling him by his military title because in England, as he explained, this privilege was reserved for officers of the highest rank. Why this did not also hold true in America, he was never asked to explain. One did not question Mr. Murdock's opinions and pronouncements. There would have been no point to it. As with a parrot, one did not talk with him, but simply received what he had to say.

My hope was to have as little to do with this strange creature as my obligation to Hart, Schaffner and Marx would allow. I was determined to find my way around London on my own terms. I spent the first night in London uneasily in the guest room of Murdock's flat on Albemarle Street. The place had a pristine opulence. Everything about it was so ostentatiously exquisite that the total effect was sickeningly vulgar. My uneasiness was compounded by Murdock's all too transparent innuendos by which he determined through my lack of response that I was indeed not one of his kind. I set out the next morning in search of quarters, and before the end of the day moved into a sparsely furnished room in a row of old frame houses a stone's throw from Piccadilly on Half Moon Street. The spartan plainness of the place was in comforting contrast to the unsavory elegance of Murdock's flat. Two white curtained windows looked down on the narrow street and gave the room a softly pleasant light. A gaunt looking iron bedstead stood in one corner. There were a couple of ancient chairs, one stiff and straight backed placed next to the bed and the other, a low slung upholstered affair, at the side of a tiny fireplace that bravely tried but failed to heat the place. A sturdy round table in the center of the room completed the furnishings. I found it all enchanting and happily settled in.

I believe that an early entry in my notebook recorded a magical occurrence that took place on the doorstep as I started out that first evening in search of dinner. I mentioned this experience earlier in this chronicle but it bears repeating, for it was one of those unforgettable happenings that appear out of nowhere and leaves behind a sense of having learned something never before known; I was shown a miraculous instant of truth.

I remember shutting the street door behind me and confronting the dusk of the early evening. The air was cold and damp and soft to the touch. A street lamp dimly illuminated the pavement and the gray, flat-fronted houses that lined the narrow, deserted street. I started walking slowly toward the lights of Piccadilly where Half Moon Street came to a dead end. I felt very much alone as I watched a cab approach from far down the street. The silence about me was broken by my steps on the pavement and by the sputtering of an ungainly old hack. As it neared me, a nasal cockney voice rose above the other sounds, singing (I do not know what), but singing with a kind of indifferent contentment, as though everything was in its preordained and proper place. As the singer and his cab passed by, for an instant I was flooded with a sense of intimate familiarity with my surroundings. And then, as the sound of the singing trailed off behind me, the feeling of strangeness returned and I was again a foreigner in a foreign land. I was to learn much about London in the year to come, but I would never regain the knowingness of this magic instant. It has never left me.

The casual yet overwhelming presence of the past impressed itself on my consciousness wherever I turned those first days in London. Everything, the buildings, whether large or small, the streets and the shops, the lampposts, the old squares and parks, even the ancient taxi cabs, seemed not the anachronisms of days dead and gone, but a vigorous, temporal amalgam of both yesterday and today. History seemed amazingly alive and well. It was inescapably everywhere. I felt at once a strange affinity that I had never before had for any city, even for Chicago where I had grown up. I was discovering the friendly face of antiquity and soon was more at home in the dingy streets of London than I ever was among the skyscrapers of New York. Was I being reminded of the ageless simplicities of Highbelow and enjoying a nostalgic association with something long known but recently forgotten?

Is there anyone who escapes the self-dissecting conflict between what is sought and what is confronted? One's own free will is eventually met by a counter will, imposing alien demands that must either be dealt with or circumvented. I have always been conscious of being victimized by the collision of these two relentlessly aggressive but mutually exclusive life forces. One arises from within, and the other attacks from without, the one an inner desire, the other an imposed imperative. Nothing could have been more perversely incompatible than the aimless freedom of my private world and the ostentatious absurdity of Murdock's world of fashion.

Murdock conducted his business in a suite of offices in an old but respectable building on Conduit Street. He was attended by two young women whom he treated like ladies in waiting and who responded efficiently, and even affectionately, to his every whim. My place in the scheme of things had, no doubt, been a worry to them. A small table in the corner of the outer office had been cleared for me with an uncomfortable tall backed chair in front of it. On my first day, Murdock, after introducing me to the ladies, led me into his inner office and settled into a commodious chair behind an enormous antique desk while I took the guest chair opposite him.

And then he proceeded to let me know that he hoped I would find ways to occupy myself usefully, as he would have little time to spare for me. I was quick to assure him that he need not worry and that I would try my best not to be a nuisance. It was agreed that I would report to the office every morning. To what end it was not decided, and as far as I can remember never was. What I did in that office, besides write letters to friends and partake of four o' clock tea, I have no recollection.

There had been a general understanding between my American employers (I received $25.00 a week) and my English overlord that I was to be exposed to the cultural and sartorial superiorities of the British environment, which in some mysterious way would replace the innocent crudities of my American background with the polished and sophisticated appearance and outlook of an English gentleman. How precisely this was to be done in terms of office routine and daily chores was left to Murdock who, as it turned out, had no idea what to do with me, aside from taking me to his tailor and fitting me out with more clothes than I could wear, some of which I did not even care to be seen in. (I remember one double-breasted suit with voluminous curving lapels that made me look like a swollen-chested bird in flight.)

After my wardrobe was completed, and for the most part permanently stored away in my closet, there was nothing further that Murdock could suggest. He was obviously greatly relieved when I let him know that I was delighted to be left to my own devices and that I would, from time to time, report to him on the progress of my British indoctrination. And so began a year of exploration and discovery that I will always remember with pleasure.

My wanderings about the city were without plan or guidance. After first making an appearance at the office, I would set out each day happily and aimlessly follow my nose to see where it would lead me. After these many years, I can recall only scattered impressions of all that my senses so eagerly absorbed as I walked up one street and down another, through lovely parks and gardens, or perhaps coming unexpectedly upon the embankment of the Thames, the Houses of Parliament or Westminster Abbey, only to climb up a narrow, alley-like street emerging on the Strand with its crowds and traffic, and then finding a restful seat on the edge of the fountain at Trafalgar Square, or perhaps a bench along the elegant expanse of Pall Mall with its broad vista reaching through Green Park to the Palace grounds. Inevitably, I would find my way to the mansions of Park Row and then through Hyde Park to Hyde Park Corner where I would listen to the street orators and the jibes and shouted replies of the listeners.

It was not long before I found my way to the British Museum. The great ethnographical collections of primitive and archaic civilizations revived the visual interests aroused in New York by my work with Morris Crawford. Here was a vista of historical treasures that dwarfed the collections that had fascinated me in New York. I spent whole days absorbing the stone carvings and paintings of Ancient Egypt, the carvings and colossal sculptures of the Mayan civilization of Central America, and the wood carvings and artifacts of the South Pacific peoples. The book shelf in my room was soon laden with the illustrated guide books and catalogues to the various collections. These works were filled with scholarly descriptions and research relating to the many exhibits, but I found myself ignoring the texts, while I would spend whole evenings examining the photographs and diagrams.

I was particularly fascinated by the symbolic language of the ancient Egyptians inscribed on sepulchral tablets and royal sarcophagi, how pictures were made to represent ideas such as a wall leaning on one side conveying the idea of falling, or a man holding a jug on his head meaning "to carry." I discovered how representations of objects and things had been finally abstracted into an alphabet of simplified linear images called hieroglyphs and how these were combined in ways to express ideas such as a double line representing the sky with a star suspended from it giving the meaning of night. The way these ideographs, as they were called, added complex meanings to the intrinsic grace and beauty of the drawn forms excited my interest and I filled many pages of a notebook with copied notations. I even acquired a little book on Egyptian grammar and came to recognize the meaning of certain symbols on sight.

Looking back upon these exploratory excursions into the art and culture of ancient civilizations, I recall that while I responded with a spirited and even inspired interest, I was somewhat troubled and puzzled by the aimlessness and disorderliness of my involvement. I did not think of myself as a particularly gifted person in the visual sense. I was, of course, aware of sharp and exciting sensory responses to the great artifacts that I found in such profusion at the British Museum, but the affinities that I felt remained passive and ineffectual. Hidden in all I saw were powerful human forces that were shaped, carved and woven into expressive forms and images. I was deeply moved by all that I saw but I did not know why. My own sense of identity was far removed from this wildly alive world, and I moved through it without really possessing it.

I had yet to discover who I was and what I might one day find the courage and will to undertake. I needed the impetus of a compulsion to act, to use my own inventive powers, to discover forms and images of my own, to draw, to shape, to form. But who was I to presume to enter into and become part of this magic world? Here I was, a half-educated, unskilled, well dressed, well fed college dropout whose life's work was to be the manufacture and sale of men's clothing. The two worlds I inhabited, as I was to discover much later, could not coexist. One day, I would admit to myself how

117

hopelessly antithetical they were, but not until I had tried, with a kind of quixotic naiveté, to reconcile the two.

I remember being particularly interested in how forms of animal life, in many cases the objects of sacred worship, appeared in primitive pictorial art; how the images of the crocodile in New Guinea and the alligator in Panama were simplified and abstracted through an evolution of stages, each stage showing a simplification of the previous stage until the design became almost totally abstracted from the original form, becoming finally wholly conventionalized with hardly a trace of even a symbolic relationship to the animal from which it derived. The notes of my observations traced many instances of such design evolution, especially in New Guinea, where the marvelously carved canoe paddles, for example, carried recognizable images of birds' heads, usually centered. Then, on the same carving, the artist would conventionalize the beaks into looped coils or scrolls that could best be accommodated by the particular size and shape of the paddle. The ingenuity and sheer ornamental skill of the New Guinea sculptors left a deep impression on me.

In the light of these exciting revelations, considerations involving the men's clothing industry, by comparison, bored and depressed me. Still, I could not ignore the fact that I had allowed my patrons to presume that I was acting in good faith and that I was seriously concerned with preparing to be of some use to them. It was out of a sense of guilt, then, that I contrived an ingenious plan to somehow subject the design of manufactured men's clothing to the improbable influence of the primitive art I had been studying. Of course, my idea took the courage of its initiative from the teachings and preachings of one M.D.C. Crawford, and it was with the assumed encouragement of the master that I plunged recklessly into what I was sure would turn out to be a hopelessly quixotic project. Yet somehow or other, I meant to have both sides of the coin on the same face, and much to my surprise, I almost succeeded. At least I found the game fascinating, while at the same time, I could live with the illusion that I was earning my weekly paycheck.

My plan involved the following considerations: The clothing firm of Hart, Schaffner and Marx had been known throughout the many years of its existence for the solid, down-to-earth quality of its mass-produced, inexpensive coats and suits, which it turned out in vast quantities. It was probably the largest and most successful manufacturer in its field and its name had become a kind of symbol of the cheap but respectable "ready-to-wear" that men of moderate means set aside for holidays and occasions. Until now, the Hart, Schaffner and Marx product never tried to invade the status conscious domain of the custom tailored man. There was nothing exclusive about a Hart, Schaffner and Marx suit. It came with two pairs of pants, and was the essence of the democratic ideal of social uniformity and individual anonymity. It was my uncle Alexander M. Levy who set out to change all this, with the help of such individuals as Captain Jack Murdock. My plan was devised in the hopes of contributing my small share to this worthy effort.

Was not my very presence in England an expression of this corporate climb up the ladder from the factory slums on the fringe of Chicago's Loop to the fashionable heights of the gentlemen's tailoring establishments centered in Bond Street in the heart of Mayfair, the cradle of Anglo-Saxon snobbishness? Would not a project expressing this aspiration be welcomed by the powers that be, and especially by my uncle, who I now realized was personally in the throes of a deep-seated anglomania? I pictured his elaborately British-cut, impeccably tailored presence leading his drably dressed horde of followers and underlings out of the offices and workrooms of Hart, Schaffner and Marx into a realm of dazzling sartorial elegance. I pictured him taking them out of the commonplace world of two pants suits, upward to the white tie and tails of the haughty Beau Brummel tradition. The vehicle I chose as my contribution to the great metamorphosis, was to be a booklet illustrating a series of specially designed suiting fabrics that I would call "Mayfair Corners."

My plan followed precisely the logic of the situation just described. I assumed that Mayfair, as a district, would be recognized at once as the traditional symbol of British social superiority and I meant to put great emphasis on this. A map would show the linear configurations of ancient parks and squares and the intersections of narrow, winding streets and broad avenues. With the help of the Baedeker guide to London, which I always carried with me on my walking tours, I could locate points on the map with the required snob appeal, such as the mansions on Curzon Street where it points in the direction of Park Lane and where the great balls and fashionable gatherings of the Regency Period took place. I marked off lovely eighteenth-century Berkeley Square, with its stately row of elegant ancient houses facing and surrounding the verdure of a tiny park. There was Green Park and Buckingham Palace, and of course the residence on St. James where the young Prince of Wales held forth, he being a personage whom Jack Murdock conceded was the best dressed man in the world after himself.

A typical page in the booklet I envisioned would show a photograph of the chosen landmark accompanied by a brief description of its place in the annals of the British aristocracy. Below this on the page would be a drawing of the particular linear configuration which identified its place on the map of May-fair. Below this drawing would be a photograph of a woven fabric which I would design, using the drawing as the basic module, repeating itself into what I hoped would be an appealing pattern that could be made into a man's suit of clothes. The fact that I had never tried my hand at textile design did not discourage me in the slightest. The fitting together of repeats of the same geometric configuration in all directions ad infinitum seemed a simple matter. I was as innocently self-confident of success as I was that day many years before when I'd approached the blackboard of my eighth grade classroom, map and crayon in hand to freehand a mural size rendition of it. I was no more surprised then, at the success of the map, than I was certain now of completing a series of designs for tweed suitings based on the map of May-fair. What I was not so sure of was the reception my project would receive from the management of Hart, Schaffner and Marx. But this did not stop me. In fact, in a strange way I found my doubts a source of encouragement.

I worked diligently on the project over a period of two months. With the help of my Baedeker, I chose a dozen or more centers of fashionable, if not historical, interest and then proceeded to put a circle around each one on a large map of the West End, as Mayfair was commonly known. I spread out on the lone table in my room, where I'd spend my evenings poring over the map extracting the exact linear formation occurring at each location, which I then proceeded to piece together in a repeating design for weaving. I found the whole process a fascinating series of visual puzzles, and each solution gave me the pleasurable satisfaction of a job well done. Each design differed from the others, thanks to the tangled, unsymmetrical way in which the ancient streets intertwined in all directions.

As I completed one design after another, I would set forth each day with a cheap camera purchased for the purpose of taking photographs of the various locations and landmarks. I was as new to the intricacies of good picture taking as to the subtleties of textile designing, but this did not seem to raise doubts that my photographs would be suitable for publications. I took snap-shots of the Park Row mansions, the Bond Street shops, Buckingham Palace, Pall Mall and the Marble Arch, Berkeley Square and all the rest from every possible angle, and in all kinds of weather. Out of the mess of prints I was able to find at least one for each subject, which, while not photographic masterpieces, were at least recognizable for what they were.

It was toward the end of April that I began to assemble the loose ends of the project and put everything together in page layouts. The only thing that was missing was the finished woven product. On each page, this was represented by a blank square marked "woven fabric." The dummy booklet was beginning to take on the look of a substantial project when word came to me through the Murdock office that Mr. and Mrs. Levy could be expected in London within a fortnight. This gave me renewed impetus to bring the whole business to completion. There were two or three photographs with which I was not satisfied and there was still a bit of polishing to do on the short descriptive paragraphs that accompanied each picture. However, I finished the thing with a few days to spare.

I had decided from the beginning, that Murdock was to know nothing of my project. Aside from sending me occasionally to the offices of the Scottish woolen mills on Golden Square to collect sample swatches of fabrics and giving me various other aimless tasks around the office, he was satisfied to let me go my own way most of the time. He must have assumed that I could not fail to absorb the benefits of the British gentleman's world if I did no more than walk up and down Bond Street each day. When I mentioned my visits to the British Museum, he was not overly impressed, possibly because it was beyond the limits of the West End. Bloomsbury, in Murdock's mind, was a foreign country and I'm sure he had never set foot in the British Museum. At any rate, I was anxious to keep his nose out of my work on Mayfair Corners because I was certain that he would have either tried to take over the idea or some version of it or, more likely, discredit it as an absurdity. As long as I remained a harmless American tourist vaguely in search of cultural polish, I was no threat to him. What I was secretly involved in was far too serious a matter and no doubt would have constituted, in his mind, an invasion of his domain. I was sure, and was later confirmed in the conviction, that he could not afford to tolerate any useful contribution that I might make through his office, and far from encouraging such a thing, he would have managed in some way to obstruct it.

As I look back from this distance in time, I am not sure whether I took more satisfaction in the excellence (as I saw it) of my achievement as a designer, or in the cleverness of the plan as an effective advertisement concocted to increase the sales of Hart, Schaffner and Marx clothing. In any case, I was wildly curious to see the reception my good uncle would give the results of my efforts.

They arrived one rainy day at Paddington Station where Murdock and I were standing side by side to welcome them. After greetings and handshakes and a dutiful kiss from me on the heavily perfumed cheek of little

Aunt Hana, they were ushered with all their luggage into an enormous black Daimler limousine, which, with its uniformed chauffeur, was to be at their service night and day for the duration of their visit. After arranging to meet them in their suite at the Ritz-Carlton at seven for cocktails and dinner, they disappeared into the commodious luxury of the Daimler's back seat, leaving us standing on the pavement looking, as I thought, very foolish.

Later that night when I returned to my room after a pompously served and ostentatiously exquisite dinner, I realized that I would have to bide my time until a moment could be found for a private talk with Uncle Al. His time would be filled with a prearranged schedule of appointments and meetings, luncheon engagements and shopping tours. For the first few days, I was to see him only under the ever present shadow of Murdock, who behaved in his presence like a fluttery dowager with a daughter to marry off. It was not until the fourth day when, upon emerging from the inner office with Murdock on his heels, he stopped by the table where I was sorting out fabric samples and commanded me to join him and Aunt Hana for tea at four o' clock sharp. He left without waiting for an answer. This, I understood, was no invitation. It was an order.

I had assumed that Captain Jack (as Uncle Al called him, continuing to use the military title, much to Murdock's embarrassment, I believe) would be on hand for Aunt Hana's tea party as usual, but to my surprise, and relief, the three of us were alone when the *maitre d'hotel* seated us at a flower bedecked table in the middle of the elegant dining room. The tea was ordered with slow, magisterial pomposity by Uncle Al, after giving due deference to Aunt Hana's wishes. When this was done, he turned to me with raised eyebrows and a suppressed grin and said, "Well, Robert, what have you got to say for yourself?"

Well, I found suddenly I had not very much to say for myself. I explained that while every effort had been made to provide me with office chores, the efficiency of the two young ladies on Murdock's staff left nothing of any consequence for me to do. The girls were hard put to find tasks for me and it seemed that everyone was relieved when I took my leave of them every morning shortly after ten o' clock, not to return until tea time at four. I described with some enthusiasm my fascination with the various London museums and art galleries, and I dwelt rather longer than I intended on the British Museum. And then I explained my intrigue with the woven and carved ornamentation of primitive tribes and cultures and the magnificence of the museum's vast collections. I found myself describing at great length the derivation and skillful abstraction of the designed figurations in all instances from forms in nature such as birds, snakes, alligators, or the human face and form, all of which were objects of fear, admiration or religious worship.

As I followed this line of thought, I found that it carried me logically to the heart and soul of the Hart, Schaffner and Marx product, the heart being a bolt of woven cloth and the soul its prestige as a commodity serving the social and physical vanity of men. It was at this point that I introduced the subject of my secret project.

After explaining that I had thought it best not to bother Murdock with the many problems which the idea involved, I told the whole long story of how and why Mayfair Corners had preoccupied me through most of the last two months. I told how I had utilized the streets and historical landmarks of fashionable Mayfair, much as the New Guinea wood carver utilized animal images in the design of his canoe paddle. After a time, I could not help but notice the change that came over Uncle Al. When I had first begun describing my daily doings and wanderings, he seemed to follow my dissertation from a distance with mild amusement and interest. I noticed a slight change in his attitude when I first mentioned an involvement in an independent project, and by the time I finished he made no attempt to conceal a now avidly aroused curiosity to see what I had done. Within a half hour, the three of us were climbing the barren stairway to my second floor room on Half-Moon Street.

There was something positively greedy about the way Uncle Al silently examined every detail of the work spread out on the table. He read each descriptive paragraph slowly and aloud — "And it was here at Devonshire House on Curzon Street that Lady Stanley presided over her famous drawing room gatherings, at which the Prince Regent was an habitué and Beau Brummel and his set were in constant attendance." Each page carried similar short descriptions celebrating the fashionable snobbishness of the British Aristocracy. There was very little writing, but what was said was enough for Uncle Al. His eyes fairly blazed with pleasure, which immediately induced dutifully enthusiastic smiles and head noddings from Aunt Hana.

After carefully thumbing through each page, he turned to examine the large, diligently worked out drawings I had made for each fabric. It was the technical workability of these designs that caused me most concern, for I wasn't sure that I'd properly constructed the repeating patterns to the limitations of the machine looms that would convert them into bolts of woven cloth. To my relief, this did not seem to worry Uncle Al, who was apparently accustomed to having the entire apparatus of his great company turn to at his command and somehow overcome any obstacles that might stand in the way of successfully carrying out his wishes. He let me know that he was very pleased with the whole plan and assured me that the fabrics would be woven and tailored into suits and trousers (not pants, mind you) and the booklet published and distributed by the onset of the Fall season. The entire project was then assembled and wrapped into a neat package which Uncle Al tucked under his arm and carried with him down the stairs and eventually all the way back to Chicago where everything was done exactly as the man predicted by the end of September.

Of course, I had never expected such complete and uncritical acceptance of the thing. I had thought that there surely would be errors and subsequent changes and alterations, and while I had been quite sure of a mild, general interest in the plan, I had not anticipated that it would be swallowed hook, line, and sinker. As a matter of fact, I thought that Uncle Al had let a certain wishful enthusiasm unhinge his practical judgment and I was quite convinced that when he confronted the practical men who would have to materialize my pretty ideas into hard actualities, he would meet with insurmountable difficulties. However, I was glad to let well enough alone and enjoy my success as long as it lasted.

Murdock, as was to be expected, was upset that such a successful undertaking had been completed under his nose without his knowledge, and he chided me with an air of wounded petulance for not letting him in on it. I watched him as Uncle Al explained the project to him in the office the next day, and it was obvious that he did not understand what it was all about. The Captain, in spite of his fine airs, was a simple-minded fellow after all.

The Levys departed and thereafter Murdock never mentioned the subject of Mayfair Corners. I don't remember a single comment from him, not even when the booklet was printed and distributed and the fabrics woven and merchandised. In fact, from this time on, he seemed to lose what little interest he did have in my apprenticeship. I continued to follow the formalities of reporting in every morning and stopping by for tea in the afternoon. But for the rest of my stay in England, I was for all practical purposes, my own keeper and a free man.

It was about this time that I took two weeks to enjoy myself making the rounds of museums, restaurants, and nightclubs in Paris, the latter in the hilariously cheerful company of my friend Andrew Goodman, who was serving an apprenticeship similar to mine with the house of Jean Patou, the famous couturier. (This education was in preparation for his subsequent career as head of the fashionable New York firm of Bergdorf Goodman.) Andrew, unlike me, managed over the years to finish what he had started with brilliant success.

On my return to London I moved to new quarters in an ancient three-storied house on a narrow, cobbled street that sloped steeply downhill from the noisy traffic of the Strand to a small, quiet park on the Thames embankment. My flat was halfway down the hill and consisted of a large pleasant living room, a small bedroom alcove, and a bathroom with a great out-sized bath tub. The living room looked out on the street, curiously named York Buildings, through three very tall windowed doors, each of which gave on a minuscule wrought iron balcony. The furnishings, while not luxurious, were more comfortable and attractive than what I'd had on Half Moon Street. To my delight, it included an old grand piano with its graceful contours accented by the soft light from the tall windows which fronted it. The rent included the valet services of the landlord, a pleasant but rather formal fellow who politely imposed on me a morning routine that included what, to him, were obviously necessary proprieties to be followed by young bachelor gentlemen. I was awakened with a cup of hot tea at seven-thirty each morning, which was slowly absorbed in bed while the tub in the adjacent bathroom was filled with steaming water. Towels and shaving equipment were neatly laid out. The man even unscrewed the cap to my toothpaste so that the open tube would be ready for squeezing.

These proceedings appeared to me, at first, to be thoroughly silly, but I soon began to enjoy the attentions and ended by taking them for granted. Each day after my bath I would emerge in my bathrobe to a delicious breakfast of eggs, bacon, and coffee laid out for me with a copy of *The London Times* on a small table in the living room. I attribute my lifelong weakness for these kinds of morning luxuries to my three months' sojourn on York Buildings. Though I was never to enjoy similar services again, I look back on them with an absurd nostalgia which has never left me.

Throughout the spring and early summer, I found that my new surroundings provided a delightful existence. As the days lengthened, I would walk along the embankment in the evenings and return to my rooms at dusk when I would settle down to the many new interests that were beginning to preoccupy me more and more. I was never without music of one sort or another, and my small phonograph was constantly playing recordings of Stravinsky ballets, Beethoven or Tchaikovsky symphonies, or the latest popular tunes from America. I began to explore the keyboard of my new piano and discovered strange chords and melodic progressions that so surprised and delighted me that I engaged a piano instructor recommended by a store dealing in musical instruments and publications. My teacher was a gentle, elderly man whose knowledge and skill seemed to me exceptional. His clothes were shabby, and he was obviously not very well off, but he took a great interest in my efforts, eventually leading me into elementary problems of harmony and composition. Before long, I was able to do a credible rendering of a part of one of Mozart's very early sonatas, which gave me a wonderful sense of achievement.

This was a period of exciting discoveries. I read prodigiously and absorbed everything I could find of the writings of Tolstoy, Samuel Butler, Bernard Shaw, Chekhov, and a host of others. I carried a pocket notebook with me wherever I went and was constantly jotting down random thoughts that appeared suddenly from nowhere, like magic revelations. These were the first fresh, and often confused, insights into the puzzlements and mysteries of inexperience, where one searches through the tangle of the unexplored and finally emerges with age-old answers that, in all innocence, appear as unique and unprecedented.

And finally I began to draw. Among my books were two volumes of Michelangelo and Leonardo's drawings that I had brought back from Paris. I spent hours studying these miracles of perception and sensitive draughtsmanship, and one day summoned up the courage to attempt to make a copy of Leonardo's pencil portrait of an old man. I reasoned that the image that met my eye was in truth composed of clusters of lines and areas of variously shaded grays, all of which, if minutely observed, should be possible to duplicate with a carefully controlled pencil on a page of drawing paper. I procured drawing pencils of various densities and a pad of proper drawing paper, and with great caution and slow deliberation set to work. I reasoned that if my eyes penetrated and seized upon each minute mark and determined the exact position, size, length, and lightness or darkness to be duplicated, it followed that when everything was properly set down that my drawing should exactly resemble the original. To my astonishment, this is precisely what happened.

I continued copying the masters, using the reproductions in the illustrated books and portfolios that I had begun to collect. Visits to the National and Tate Galleries gave me opportunities to study the originals. It might interest the reader to know that beginning the summer of my sixteenth birthday, my

126

good father began taking us on five successive tours of the Continent. The trips were planned with Baedeker precision to visit and view the historic art and architecture of France, Italy, Germany, Switzerland, Austria, and Belgium. But in those days I was of a mind that recalled the marvelous food at *Pre Catalin* in the *Bois de Bologne*, and tea at *Rumplemeyers* on the *Rue Rivoli* more clearly than the great paintings of the Louvre. I remember the magnificent accommodations at the *Hotel Excelsior* on the Lido outside of Venice before the art treasures of the *Doges Palace*; the race track at *Ostend* more clearly than the great collections of Flemish painting in Brussels. In London in 1927, it seemed to me that I was confronting art for the first time.

In the beginning, my interest centered in the subtle intangibles of characterization and facial expression, which reflected a tendency to see the drawings as descriptive adjuncts to literary concepts. But soon, I became more and more responsive to the structural aesthetic of textural and linear realities alone and was able to enjoy simultaneously, yet separately, the satisfactions of sheer, masterly draughtsmanship and the delights of penetrating insights into human nature that the marvelously drawn heads and faces induced.

After a time I became conscious of what had been a lifelong habit of staring at people, which now became deliberate and purposeful. I fell into the habit of memorizing the contours and general structure of a particular face that might catch my eye in a crowded bus or while holding onto a strap in the underground railway. Upon returning to my desk, I would try to revive whatever fragments of the original observation remained visibly alive in my memory and set them down on paper. One evening, on the strength of these efforts, I decided to recall whatever I could from the image of my father's face when I thought of him several thousand miles away vacationing with my sister in California. I was quite happy with the drawing that resulted, which indeed carried a distinct likeness, in spite of the awkwardness of the draughtsmanship. From then on, until I took up sculpture in earnest a year or so later, I drew an endless series of human heads and faces, mostly of my own invention—out of nowhere, so to speak. It became a kind of obsession.

At this point, I want to return to the subject of music. For it was through music, rather than visual art or literary forms, that I first experienced awareness of that overpowering sense of an all-embracing unity that emerges from the structural progressions of the smaller tangible parts of a great work of art. Since the age of fifteen, when the two brilliant sons of piano virtuosi Fanny Bloomfield Zeisler, Paul and Earnest, introduced me to the mysteries of classical musical forms, I had turned to music more and more for the deep, but not very well understood, pleasure it gave me. I owned a portable phonograph that required constant cranking and repeated changing of the steel needles that produced scratchy, unnatural sounds, which today would seem intolerable, but at the time was more than adequate. My grasp of the sophisticated forms, which I listened to over and over until I was able to anticipate every audible phrase, was entirely a matter of sense perception. Intellectually I was, and have remained, ignorant of the rationale of musical structure and composition or of the language of musical analysis. My friend, the piano instructor, tried to provide a better understanding of the sound sequences and arrangements that gave me such pleasure but without much success.

As recently as some ten years ago, I shocked the chairman of the music department at Brooklyn College by insisting that I could listen as intelligently as he to the Mahler First Symphony with only the auditory sense-perception I was born with. It seemed to him that what I heard in my ignorance was quite different from what was received by his educated ear, and that what I was quite literally doing was whistling in the dark. I could not convince him that the great structural unities that are the essence of aesthetic perception and realization can be grasped and embraced by the senses without the help of the analytical mind. I do not deny that a great piano virtuoso, no doubt by combining analytical knowledge with profound sense-response and perception, enjoys more monumental musical experiences than I, but I deny that my enjoyment of the great works is no more than a form of musical idiocy.

I first became aware of great compositional unities in music when I encountered the ballets of Stravinsky during the period of my sojourn at York Buildings. At the suggestion of something read in a newspaper, or overheard in a restaurant or on a bus, I purchased a balcony reservation for a performance of *The Fire Bird* by Diaghelev's famous company with the composer conducting. Seated in the balcony's front row in the very center of the auditorium, I had a marvelously unobstructed view of the entire orchestra, and the full expanse of the huge stage. I recall this fact because from the moment the house was darkened and the curtain raised, I lost awareness of my actual surroundings and entered another world. The presence of the audience, the theatrical aspects of the spectacle disappeared, and I became a living part of the magical garden where a handsome prince was united with his lovely Fire Bird. For the first time in my life, I experienced the perfect union of haunting musical sound, expressive painted imagery, and the exquisite choreography of human bodies in motion.

This image of a singular, all embracing unity crystallized from a conglomerate reality of disparate and often conflicting parts, came to me for the first time on seeing and hearing *The Fire Bird*. I was totally unprepared for this kind of transcendent experience, and at the end when the curtain fell I was shocked and embarrassed to find my face wet with tears. I knew that I had not been sentimentally affected by the romantic fairy tale. For I had all but ignored the storybook aspects of the action for its sheer sensory impact. It was something else that had moved me so profoundly. I could not explain it, but I knew I had had a rare and overwhelming experience.

This was the beginning. Over the years the search for this image of unity has gone on. I have found it in painting, in philosophical speculation, in music and literature, and in controlled but expressive patterns of human relationships and every day life. It is the source of hope and optimism, and the will to live.

(from collected notes)

The coherence of controlled order and immutable variety is so organic that without it, diversity degenerates into disorder, and unity into mere tidiness.

Truth is diversity. Discipline is unity. Truth and discipline are essentially incompatible and can be combined into a positive force only by extraordinary exertions of human will and intelligence. Hence the predominance in human affairs of fragmented truths and artificial unities.

🔲 🔲 🔲

WHAT HAS BEEN WRITTEN so far, must surely give the impression of a solitary, introspective life devoted to matters of the mind and spirit and indifferent to the common pleasures and amenities of conventional existence. It is true that I made few friends, tending to protect my freedom of thought and movement by avoiding the company and companionship of others and the give and take of obligations that go with even the simplest of social activity. It is also true that at the age of twenty-two, I was a totally self-centered young man intent upon preventing the world about him from making demands that would disturb the solitary remoteness of an untouchable privacy. I was fully aware of the nature of my need and filled my notebooks with efforts to explain it to myself.

Still, I was by no means a hermit following a path of ascetic self-denial. In fact, I was somewhat of a hedonist and indulged myself in the good and pleasant things of life as far as means allowed. I enjoyed the London theater and the pleasure of dining at many of the West End's excellent restaurants. I was rather vain about my appearance and readily fell in line with the West End custom of wearing a dinner jacket and top hat for most evening occasions. There was nothing unusual those days to see people in silk hats and evening gowns crowding into packed underground trains on their way to theater or a dinner rendezvous. I was quite happy to be a part of this well-mannered, good-humored crowd, and my enjoyment was doubled by the fact that, being always alone, there was nothing to distract me from observing and absorbing everything within sight or earshot. I was a thoroughly appreciative audience to the life that swirled about me. Though I was without friends or companionship, I was probably the least lonely young man in London.

🔲🔲🔲

(from notes)
WHAT AM I?

What am I when I speak to you?
Myself?
Or a clownish presence
Spawned by the cruel possessiveness
Of words.

🔲🔲🔲

I RECOGNIZE IN THE ATTITUDES and inclinations of young people today, my own refusal to believe in the integrity, or even the reality, of my relationship to the society into which I was born. In the course of this rambling discourse, I am inclined to lose awareness of my Highbelovian origins and am only reminded of them when certain conditions of life on this earth are so obviously comparable to that other, lost existence that reference to it is inescapable. I am certain that the almost universal compulsion of the earthbound young to break away from artificial and unnatural ways of living and doing, mandated by rigid conventions inherited from the past, is an instinct carried into this life from that other world where integrity of mind and spirit is a common birthright, not an exclusive attribute of saints and martyrs. For as I remember, the Highbelovian young set the example for the old, who tended to be corrupted by the passing years. Highbelovians honored the incorruptible moral innocence of children and the immunity of youth to diseases of the spirit and illnesses of character. By contrast, the children of mortal men are in constant revolt against the insistence of their elders that they discard their inherited virtues and replace them with the conventional aims and outlook of an adult society suffering from what my Highbelovian records would describe as the unsavory, if not fatal, afflictions which were known as *looking forward with anxiety, looking back with longing* or *regret, looking up with humility,* and *looking down with pride.* Though my rebellion as a youth of twenty-two was mild and ineffective compared to the war being waged by the young people of today (1973), in my own way I fought the age-old battle for the right to be young and of free mind and spirit. I was, in spite of the pressures of contrary circumstances, affirming my Highbelovian heritage.

Perhaps it was not so much a battle that was fought, as a disengagement, a breaking off of diplomatic relations, so to speak. The few attempts that I made to come to terms with my fellow humans and join them in common forms of social intercourse were in each case abandoned after a brief but futile effort. In one way or another, by accident or through acquaintances from America, I came into contact with friendly people, both English and American, who were all too willing that I join them in their social activities. The fact that I can recall but one or two people indicates how feebly I responded to their friendliness.

I remember a round-faced, rather jolly middle-aged fellow who struck up a conversation with me on the Channel boat returning from France, and who upon landing, urged me to get in touch with him at his home in London, presenting me with a card indicating that he was a titled gentleman, a Sir Arthur something-or-other with a "Bart." at the end. After a week or two, out of sheer curiosity, I wrote him a note and received in answer an invitation to dinner and theater. As it happened, both he and his wife, a nondescript woman about whom I can recall nothing, were hospitable and friendly. Yet, in spite of my efforts to respond in kind, I found myself unable to suppress an ever-mounting sense of painful incompatibility, until, by the end of the evening I could hardly hide my discomfort behind a grimly smiling mask of empty good manners which I somehow managed to wear to the end. Why these good people ever bothered to approach me again, I cannot understand. Within a week, I received a letter from the lady inviting me to a dinner party. A letter, which I am ashamed to admit, was not given the consideration of a reply. As I have said, mine was a disengagement. I did not fight. I retreated. Or perhaps I should say, I retired from the scene of battle.

Then there was that other attempt to join the ranks of conventional society. At someone's suggestion, I believe it was one of the secretaries in Murdock's office, I joined the English Speaking Union. This was, as I soon discovered, a great mistake.

Almost everything about my brief connection with the English Speaking Union has been mercifully forgotten, save for a few unfortunately unforgettable details. I remember being enthusiastically welcomed into the fold by an aggressive little woman in tweeds exuding a muscular dynamism so formidably friendly that what was meant to be a warm and reassuring greeting became a frightening frontal attack against which, under the circumstances, there was no defense. I was shown about the premises, an old but stately building (if I remember correctly) following in the wake of the lady's high spirits like a puppet on a string. After settling the details of my induction into the organization, I was loaded down with an armful of pamphlets and brochures explaining the many benefits of membership and the worthiness of the cause of eternal friendship between all the English speaking people on earth. Upon leaving I was admonished, rather than invited, to attend an informal party to be given for the members and their friends the forthcoming Saturday night.

Although I approached this affair with definite misgivings, I told myself that I might find a way here of breaking out of my self-imposed isolation and so give myself the pleasures and distractions of normal social intercourse. As it turned out, I could not have chosen a more effective way of further alienating myself from the gregarious aspects of life on this earth. As I entered the building on that fateful Saturday evening, I was immediately confronted by one of the many formidable ladies young and old who were standing about. As a new member, I was immediately seized upon and steered about the place, completely powerless to do anything but grin foolishly as I was introduced to everyone, shaking one hand after the other in that hearty, single-stroke British greeting that all but jerks one's arm from its socket. I remember how a kind of numbness gradually overcame my sensibilities. The occasion and all its people became for me a ridiculously staged pantomime of some kind of unidentifiable reality.

As the evening proceeded I found myself conversing idiotically with one group after the other, inanely answering questions about my origins and interests, and my opinions of this and that until I heard myself say almost anything that came to mind whether it was true or not. A kind of quiet hysteria took hold of me, culminating in a wild half-dance/half-game where everyone in the place joined hands and tramped about to an insane musical rhythm banged out from an untuned piano. I was swirled about in a line following a snakelike pattern, which broke up into smaller lines of people jumping and leaping and finally running hand-in-hand, side-by-side, to some kind of shouted command screamed out by whoever was in charge of the strange maneuvers. I remember, as in a bad dream, the perspiring, grimly laughing, wide-eyed excitement in the faces that flashed by me as the lines corkscrewed past each other. I remember wondering how these otherwise sane and sober people had catapulted a simple evening's entertainment into the wildly gy- rating illusion of a collective nightmare. I remember releasing myself from the wet hands that gripped mine from both left and right of me as our end of the line was passing the open door that led to the large reception hall, through which I rather flew than walked, stopping only for my coat and hat. The raucous piano banging followed me to the street where I struck out on the run to leave the English Speaking Union forever far behind.

In reviving these long ago days and bringing to life again the person that I remember first as a child, then a boy, and finally as a young man, I have to remind myself that this fellow is indeed the same one who sits here writing these words. Though there is an interval of forty-six years between my Eng- lish sojourn and this year of 1973, and in some respects the young man and the old man appear to be of different worlds, in other, perhaps truer ways, we remain changelessly identical. There has been a constant and dominant inner existence in perpetual confrontation with an ever-changing reality, tol- erating at times a fragilely contrived compatibility, but for the most part re- maining profoundly alienated. It seems I have always been aware of a perceptive and comprehending sensory intelligence existing and operating in total isolation, generating its own vitality, creating and nurturing its own knowledgeability, discovering its own truth within its own sense of being, stubbornly unresponsive to the prejudiced truths of the outer world.

I have often questioned whether painting is indeed my true calling, consid- ering how, for the first twenty years of my life, I was almost totally without the visual self-consciousness of the "born" artist, and considering that I did not se- riously begin to draw and model in clay or to identify myself to myself as an artist until the age of twenty-three. Then, even as now, there seemed to be lit- tle connection between the given, conceptual world of men and the innocently found world of self. Awareness of this split has always been painfully present, even in earliest childhood. I felt it keenly throughout a slow intellectual awak- ening and remained unrelieved in later years by a purely heuristic order of knowledge derived from fragments of truth found, revealed, and resolved out of the chaos of a self-contained and almost uneducable inner existence.

This is not to say that I was not profoundly influenced by the insights of writers and thinkers such as Dostoevsky (*The Brothers Karamazov*), Tolstoy (*Childhood, Boyhood and Youth*), Samuel Butler (*The Note Books, Evolution Old and New, Luck or Cunning, The Way Of All Flesh*), Henri Bergsen (*Elan Vital*), Bernard Shaw (*The Prefaces*), and many others. Yet, it always seemed that what they set before me was not new and untasted knowledge, but a kind of miraculous clairvoyance into my own, as yet unresolved, existence. It was as though by some unaccountable coincidence, their words confirmed and crystallized what I already knew without knowing that I knew it.

In London, the outer world appeared as a series of staged locales, a conglomeration of shifting scenes, one dissolving into the other in a symmetrically repetitious time continuum, peopled with hordes of anonymous human forms and faces swarming endlessly before my eyes like a performance without plot or purpose. Now and then, when a person here or there stepped off this stage and approached the boundaries of my private world, I would cautiously reach out to touch our shared reality, only to find that in doing so I had left my inner self behind. At that moment, I had joined the other actors on the stage of the outer world, this time playing a fool's part in an aimless spectacle of my own contrivance.

And so I came to realize that the two worlds could not be combined without one destroying or deforming the other. I discovered that the conflict could never be entirely resolved one way or the other, and that a hostile co-existence would somehow have to be tolerated and surmounted. It was then that I found the courage to barricade my inner life from the given identities of the world into which I had been born and to find my way through the nameless realities of self. It was at this moment that I accepted the destiny and identity of a creative mind and spirit. I left the world behind by somehow putting it into a proper box and bringing it along with me.

While remaining in the nominal employ of Hart, Schaffner and Marx under the undemanding aegis of Jack Murdock, I began to write with new dedication and sense of purpose. For the first time, I dared to think of myself as a writer like other writers, as a man with something to say. Thoughts and insights and ideas crowded my mind and I was constantly reaching into my pocket, no matter where I happened to be, for one of the little leather notebooks that I filled one after the other with scrawlings and reminders of little insights I knew would be lost forever if trusted to memory. Evenings, I would expand these jottings into long entries in my journal. I managed to fill the pages of several of these larger notebooks (now destroyed) with a con-glomeration of cluttered thoughts about the human condition based on con-clusions drawn from observation of others and from self-examination. While I never consciously set out to write in the manner of authors whom I revered, such as Chekhov (translated by Constance Garnett), there was no doubt that he, as well as others, influenced the way I tried to use words and formulate thoughts.

In all innocence and with a starry-eyed fervor, I doggedly set about teaching myself to write. I had small success, for I never did acquire the professional proficiency that I sought, and today I still write with the same groping uncertainty of a beginner. The only difference is that better judg-ment in the use of words has come with experience along with a sharpened critical sense of my own limitations. When I do find that I have written a good thing, my pleasure with it is doubled by the fact that I never expected to. For me good writing per se is non-existent, for the good in it must start with whatever the writing is writing about, that is to say with the depth and breadth of the understanding and perceptivity which the words are merely conveying.

One of the art historians at Brooklyn College who I know disagreed with much that I believed in, to my annoyance would always tell me, upon hav-ing read something I had written, how well I write. I realized that he was re-ally trying not to tell me how much he disliked what I was saying by dwelling on how much he liked the way I said it. I suppose it is possible to write well about nothing or anything; but writing for its own sake as a virtue unto itself never has touched me deeply. This being so, it can be said that I am not truly a writer and I would not argue with that. I am simply trying to keep something alive that would be dead and gone without the words I write.

The life force in a created thing is its vital essence. How it is structured and ornamented and held together has validity only if it is of this essence. Lacking it, what emerges is fiddle-faddle no matter how perfectly it might be fashioned.

The inner essence of being is constantly seeking self-identity in created form. It craves transmutation from essence to substance, from the nameless to the named, from the merely mutely experienced to the articulated known. This compulsion is universal and is a crucial factor in the lives of all human beings. How it is resolved determines the quality of the existence of every man alive. The created forms and images of poets and painters and philosophers are merely symbolic concretions of this same compulsion. The great hazard here is that the created form, released from its living source, may shed the vital identities of its self-hood and then contrive to conceal the sudden emptiness within the alien identities of a ready-made outer world. This is what Morris Crawford meant when he told me not to be deceived into believing that my youthful first efforts as a writer amounted to anything more than a game of words. I was hurt and angered by this, for I could not believe that what I had so carefully structured into literate form could so obscure and falsify the source experience I was trying to project. I understand now how right he was.

I was amused to read the following quotation this morning (3/25/73) in an article on Melville in the *New York Review* by Alfred Kazin. Writing in 1848, George Templeton Strong said, "Literature pursued as an end for its own sake not for the truths of which it may be made the vehicle, is a worthless affair."[1] It has taken me too long to say as much.

There is here, of course, the threat of a take-over of one of two unacceptable extremes, the one an artless naturalism, and the other a self-enclosed and self-preening aestheticism for its own sake. I think Marcel Breuer clearly perceived the danger of a drift to one or the other end when he spoke at a symposium on the responsibility of the artist. He shied from one extreme by disclaiming, as an architect, the status of an artist, saying that his area of inventive and productive activity was essentially a matter of the human needs of every day life. He avoided the other extreme by confessing that the architectural product could end as a work of art, adding significantly that this end was less likely when the architect goes about his task self-consciously identifying it with art and was, perhaps, more likely to succeed in this respect if he applied his skill and taste to the architectural problem as a humanist rather than as an artist. It is the old thought that art is more likely to occur in the absence of calculated artfulness.

I suppose it is in the light of this understanding that I have gone to such pains to define the limitations, if not the hazards, of the written word with regard to the survival of one's own self-revealed reality. The word has to be of this reality, and in so being, we can hope that it will evolve in the form of art. This, however, can never be premeditated without not only smothering the chance of art, but also perverting the source reality to boot.

◨◨◨

(notation, May 20, 1949)

Twenty years ago I decided that words corrupted thought and that only lies could be spoken. After all these years I have progressed to the realization that it is possible to speak the unspeakable. It is not only possible, but constitutes the only good reason for taking the trouble to write at all.

(notation, undated)

The liberation of the eye depends more and more on the integrity of the word.

🔲🔲🔲

How did I ever become a painter? And why did so many years pass before I discovered what eventually became an obsessive involvement?

The first painting I ever attempted was a crude miniature landscape done of the countryside environs of Aberdeen in Scotland where I spent the summer months of 1927, supposedly to gain some knowledge of the workings of one of the large woolen mills that supplied *H.S. & M.* with fabrics.

The mill was owned by and carried the name, as I recall, of a Crombie family who had been operating the business for generations. Living quarters were found for me with an elderly couple who let a few rooms of their rambling stone house to permanent guests. All the houses in Aberdeen were made of granite, all very much alike in the gray monotony of their solid gracelessness. Was not the town called the "City of Granite"? I know for certain it was notorious for the plethora of churches built of the same gray stone which seemed to rise everywhere and anywhere one happened to look.

I settled down in a comfortable room with a bay overlooking a well-kept lawn fringed with shrubbery and flowers. The Crombie family, out of deference to their very profitable business connection with *H. S. & M.*, invited me to dinner the day of my arrival. I suffered through a never-ending evening and soon ran out of right things to say. The invitation mercifully was not repeated, though the Crombies, who were a stolidly elegant middle-aged couple, apparently kept a distant interest in my welfare through the manager of the mill who arranged a guest membership at the local golf club.

My main preoccupation in Aberdeen was supposed to center on the manufacture of woolen fabric. I was to spend a certain period of time in each process, starting, as I recall, with the carding of the wool through the weaving of the finished product. I was not fascinated with the various technologies of machined textile fabrication. Once I had understood the mechanics of each situation, there seemed to be nothing left to do but stand around staring at the monotonously rhythmic motions of the machines while being half deafened by the slam-bang clanking cacophony of ear-splitting sound that filled the endless acreage of the ancient factory. The place was badly ventilated and the summer heat added to the general discomfort. After the first few days, I began to wonder how the people who worked there, many of them since childhood, could survive with their sanity (let alone their health) intact. No one, to my astonishment, seemed to mind.

For my part, it was not long, perhaps a week, before I found myself each morning shortly after my arrival drifting unnoticed toward an inconspicuous exit, outside of which I had parked my bicycle which I would happily mount and pedal down an old road into the rolling verdure of the Scottish countryside.

It was on one of these delightful excursions when, stopping for a rest by the roadside and enjoying the details of the landscape spread before me, the thought came to me that I might try to assemble my observations into a painted reproduction. My efforts, until now, had been limited to pencil drawings, which seemed a daring enough enterprise without presuming to extend the experiment into painting with color, about which I was totally ignorant. I would not even know how to begin. However, the scene that spread out before my eyes gradually separated itself from the transitory vagaries of a traveler's passing impressions and became a fixed image demanding study and clarification. Down and across a gently sloping meadow, my eyes settled upon a cottage built of fieldstone walls and a thickset thatched roof. The place looked as though it had been spawned by the earth with a history as ancient as the enormous, wild-looking oak tree that hovered over it like a benign protector.

I did not approach the experiment with the reckless enthusiasm of the innocently hopeful beginner. There was a certain caution, an almost fearful hesitancy in starting the project. I returned day after day to my roadside observation post to stare at and study the details and configurated aspect of the cottage and its surroundings. The place seemed to be deserted. For I was never to see anyone enter or leave and the adjacent grounds were unkempt and overrun with the tall weeds of the encroaching meadow. These daily visits went on for a week or more until my eyes seemed to respond to the scene with the sense of possessive familiarity that comes with a long and intimate acquaintance.

Though I knew I would eventually take the leap and try to produce a painted image of this new reality that had become part of me, I did not worry too much about how this was to be accomplished, feeling that the practicalities of the painter's problem would somehow be overcome once my eyes knew what they were doing and seeing. One day, I finally brought some pencils and a drawing pad with me and I began to draw, not only what I was seeing but also what, through long and silent study, I knew to be there.

◨◨◨

(notation, circa 1932 {repeated})

It is not drawing from what you see but from what you have looked at that counts.

◨◨◨

FORTY-SIX SUMMERS HAVE PASSED since those long August days in the north of Scotland. I remember well at day's end the magnificent expanse of wild color and massive cloud formations that rose from the horizon and spread in all directions to cover the heavens with huge stains and streaks of blinding red and orange, fading upward into great areas of pink and violet and blue that emerged and disappeared and reemerged again from behind swiftly moving billowy mountains of white and gray. I can remember all this vividly, those fiery sunsets that persisted far into what until then had been for me the hours of night and darkness. I remember this, but I have difficulty recalling the drawings that I made for the little painting of my cottage, which I finally managed to finish.

I know, for one thing, that it did not occur to me to paint directly from observation. I acquired some tubes of oil paint, a small canvas board, and some brushes. Then using my desk as an easel, I proceeded to transfer the prepared drawing to the canvas and then apply the colors as I remembered them to the drawing. I don't know why I chose this particular procedure, but I do recall that it didn't occur to me that there might be some other and better way of attacking the problem. I was mildly pleased with the little thing that resulted. For some sentimental reason, I kept it for many years, perhaps to remind myself of my innocent beginnings. It was awkward, inept, and ugly. When I did finally destroy it I wondered why it had not persuaded me never to paint again. It was such a drab little image to have appeared in the wake of my wildly beautiful sunsets. Although I had just turned twenty-two, I was a very unsophisticated adolescent where matters of art were concerned.

I think I was as troubled then (as now) by awareness of a vast inner reservoir of inexpressible knowledge, of living in the presence of intimately known truth, an almost clairvoyant knowingness that remained fulfilling only when locked within me, hidden from the man-made world of a form and language, an undiscoverable discovery, a revelation unrevealed. What an unbridgeable chasm lay between this realm and my words and images! Throughout the years since those early efforts in London and in Scotland, there have been rare moments when an articulated thought or a painted image has touched the hidden revelation and miraculously given it life. These moments seem to happen as if by some strange and wonderful magic that circumvents the purposeful will and the calculated intention. One such moment can overpower and mitigate the failures and frustrations of a lifetime. No wonder one is forever reaching for it.

◻◻◻

TOWARD THE END OF SEPTEMBER, I returned to London to finish out the year that had been planned for me. Actually, of course, there had been no plan. My being in England was a stillborn corporate happening, the unattended and unresolved consequence of a high level executive decision about which no one had the faintest idea what to do. By the time I settled into new living quarters, I was aware that I would soon have to decide how much longer I could continue to deceive myself about my fitness for the career that lay ahead. Until now, I'd been able to persuade myself that my misgivings could be put aside, that the months ahead would give me time to find the right solution. Not so any more. Time was running out.

I know now, though I was not aware of it at the time, that I had begun taking leave of Hart, Schaffner and Marx when I left the high-toned manners and proprieties of the West End for a neighborhood of an entirely different sort. My new abode was a draughty, high-ceilinged little building in Chelsea. The place had once been a chapel but was converted to a studio by a painter who had sublet it to a young fellow of my own age whose acquaintance I had made across a library table at the British Museum. I have forgotten his name (I'll call him Sam), but I remember him rather well, for he was an excessively articulate person with the habit of never brushing his hair; he let it remain tangled and unkempt (in those days an oddity) which struck me as a ridiculous affection. He was afflicted with a lack of natural perceptivity, a kind of insight blindness, you might call it, which sometimes seems to be the curse of overbearingly bright individuals.

We were both alone in London, he involved in graduate research for an American university, and I merely in aimless exploration, to no particular purpose, of the Polynesian cultures of the South Pacific. Although we managed to meet many times thereafter for a drink or dinner, we were natural antagonists and could rarely agree on anything. Whenever we met, there was sure to be an argument. I remember one rather vividly, which went like this:

R.J.W.: You cannot discover truth with words. The only thing you can do with words is describe and identify the truth after you have found it.

Sam: I cannot think without words. Nothing exists until language rescues it from the limbo of wordlessness. I cannot conceive of a tree without the help of the word for it.

R.J.W.: Can't you just envisage the tree as though you were standing in front of it?

Sam: If the tree is not there, the word has to replace the missing reality. I can't just sit there in a trance and conjure up a tree. I can't think about nothing. Without words there is no thought. Reality is rescued from the chaos of mindlessness by language.

R.J.W: For me, words are the unreal factor. They only come to life when selected to describe an already found and known reality.

Sam: Quite the contrary. Reality has no existence until it is given one by a word.

R.J.W.: On the contrary. I find reality is more often distorted or even destroyed by a word than enhanced by it.

Sam: I admit one can choose the wrong word and, as a result, never find the truth.

R.J.W. One can choose the wrong word and lose the truth.

Sam: The trouble with you, Bob, is that you have too much imagination.

R.J.W.: The trouble with you, Sam, is not that you never had an imagination but that somewhere along the way, you traded it for a good dictionary.

Sam: You're wrong. I discovered it in a dictionary.

R.J.W.: What do you see when I say "sunset?"

Sam: I see you asking me what I see when you say "sunset."

R.J.W.: You mean, you don't see a sunset?

Sam: Of course not.

R.J.W.: What does the word sunset mean to you?

Sam: It means what it says. It means sunset.

R.J.W.: One of us must be insane.

Sam: That's what I've been thinking.

R.J.W.: You mean me?

Sam: I don't mean me.

The preceding dialogue took place forty-six years ago when I was twenty-two years old. I recalled and recorded it on Cape Cod this summer of 1973. One day, when my old friend and neighbor Gyorgy Kepes dropped by for a short visit, I read him what I'd written.

A couple of days later, I returned the visit and was sitting on the Kepes porch in the pines overlooking Long Pond when Gyuri handed me a book by his friend Gerald Holten with the title, *Thematic Origins of Scientific Thought*. I opened it to a page with a marked paragraph. He told me to read it.

"The words or the language, as they are written or spoken, do not seem to play any role in my mechanism of thought. The physical entities which seem to serve as elements in thought are certain signs and more or less clear images, which can be 'voluntarily' reproduced and combined. . . . But taken from a psychological viewpoint, this combinatory play seems to be the essential feature in productive thought—before there is any connection with logical construction in words or other kinds of signs which can be communicated to others. The above-mentioned elements are, in my case, of visual and some muscular types. Conventional words or other signs have to be sought for laboriously only in a secondary stage, when the mentioned associative play is sufficiently established and can be reproduced at will."[2]

These were the words of Albert Einstein.

With the sun low over the pond, I looked up from the book and back through the years, realizing that for the first time I'd just had the last word in the argument with Sam.

🔲🔲🔲

My friend Henry Geiger, upon reading the foregoing dialogue, wrote from California (9/11/73):

"Surely no one who has with pain searched for the right word could ever suppose that the flow of thought must be in verbal terms."

But then he goes on to explain how good writing, in revealing an already found truth, may also at the same time miraculously suggest the presence of an unexpected extension of the known into a new revelation. In short, he shows precisely how the slave of thought, the word, finally earns the right to lead the way.

"Paradoxically, it seems likely that the best use of words is able to lead the reader back to pre-verbal imagery, accomplishing a strange liberation from the mechanistic effect of syntax. I wonder if this is not the truly human quality of language—that it can be self transcending. . . ."

Some few years ago, after a lifelong distrust of verbalized thought, I entered the following caveat in my notebook:

The liberation of the eye seems to depend more and more on the integrity of the word.

I knew that what I had said was true, but I could not follow the insight through to a rationale for it. Henry Geiger had uncovered the "pre-verbal" logic of this perfectly valid conclusion that had lost contact with its own origins. Henry, in short, explained me to myself. It is the kind of thing he has been doing for people through his writing for the past twenty-five years. We owe him much.

▣ ▣ ▣

MOVING INTO A PAINTER'S STUDIO at this point, did not mean that I had begun to think of myself as an artist, or that I had decided to turn my back on the ties and commitments that still bound me to the conventional people I was supposed to be serving. I had found the place through the accident of a chance acquaintanceship. I was not charmed by it and I took it more out of curiosity than choice.

The room was long and narrow. Its gray walls rose to an ungainly height and one side was punctured by a row of tall, narrow windows. Through them, the sullen glare of true north light tried to illuminate the room, but succeeded only in dissolving into a cheerless twilight that overspread the place. Large, somber, red-brown paintings of flattened out nudes crowded the walls. The furnishing were sparse: a bulky desk, an outsized studio bed, an empty easel, a scattering of straight-back chairs, a battered old sofa, and a fireplace that refused to subdue the autumn chill. During the past year, moving from one unfamiliar setting to the next, I'd always had the happy faculty of being able to settle into strange surroundings with the comforting sense of soon feeling very much at home. Not so with the house in Chelsea. I could not take full possession of it like the others. It remained stubbornly remote and forbidding. It never seemed to be quite real and I suppose that was why I found it fascinating.

One would think that my newly awakened interest in drawing and painting would have been catalyzed into further action in the atmosphere of an artist's studio. But on the contrary, those last months, save for a few drawings, were for the most part devoted to writing and pub crawling.

My chapel was situated a stone's throw from Fulham Road. I have no idea how this particular stretch of the famous old thoroughfare has survived the years, but in the year of 1927, it could boast more public houses than any other street in London. I have forgotten the name of the street I lived on, but I remember I had but to turn left on closing my door and walk but a few hundred steps before finding myself dead ended on Fulham Road, at which point I could turn left or right and for a mile in either direction find my way into what I am sure were some of the most memorably entertaining drinking establishments to be found anywhere in the world. It is a curious and, I think, wonderful anomaly that after eight months among the British upper classes, I emerged from my anti-social shell and found the pleasures of a gregarious existence over endless glasses of excellent ale in the hilarious company of the London Cockney.

▣ ▣ ▣

As the end of my year's "education" drew near, and the job, whatever it was, that awaited me in Chicago became an imminent reality, I could no longer pretend to myself that I actually might choose to become a fixture in the men's clothing industry. I cannot recall how I managed to face up to Uncle Al with this decision, or when or where it was that I told him of it. Both he and Aunt Hana were undoubtedly fond of me, and I knew that my defection would hurt them. And although I had always felt a kind of unbending intolerance of their pretentious ways, I was aware that they had wanted to help me get a start in the world, in their world to be sure, and I had let them down. Now, after all these years, in the perspective of old age, my sympathies seem to lie not with my youthful self but with those two would-be benefactors whose good intentions toward me were never quite understood or accepted for what they were. Young men facing the open road of an unknown but beckoning destiny are apt to be cruelly intolerant of well meaning, helping hands that seem to obstruct the uncharted way.

144

I don't remember what their immediate reaction was, but they accepted what to them must have seemed a betrayal with more good grace and tolerance than I had ever shown them. Uncle Al was at heart a frustrated author and wishful intellectual. He retired within a few years from his prestigious and lucrative position at Hart, Schaffner and Marx at the age of fifty-two, to settle down on a fat annuity in California and devote himself to writing. I remember seeing them both in Chicago some few years later, on one of their visits there, when Uncle Al rather diffidently brought forth a small manuscript which he asked me to read. Unbelievably I noticed about him a painful eagerness which the old aura of authoritative arrogance from his days of executive glory could not conceal.

I found myself suddenly embarrassed and sorry for him. I had been told at the time of his retirement that his colleagues in the executive hierarchy of the corporation had pleaded with him not to give up the leadership he had so brilliantly provided. At fifty-two, he was at the very prime of his business career, and for those who had placed their trust in his abilities his resignation was an unforgivable desertion.

I took the manuscript with me and began reading it that evening. It was the beginnings of a novel. I found myself so astounded at the absurdity of the concept and the almost childlike ineptitude of the writing that I was unable, out of sheer embarrassment for the author, to finish it. And I began to ponder the coincidence of our mutual attempts at escape from the American world of practical affairs for a strange and remote world of imagination and make-believe, of literature, philosophy and art, a world that neither of us was born into but of which we both longed to be a part.

It is only at this distance that I can see that Uncle Al and I were not the cultural and spiritual antagonists I thought, but in fact were both lost souls, two fallen Highbelovians trapped in this Shrinkers' mortal hell in search of a way back to the old existence we had left behind. Uncle Al was so deeply mired in the muck of this new world that his attempt to free himself was seemingly hopeless. Looking back, I find the only difference between the two of us was that I, at the age of twenty-two, was not so far from my Highbelovian origins or so thoroughly corrupted by my Highbelovian after-life that the way back to Nirvana was at least not totally blocked.

I have not seen the Levys since their visit to Chicago. At the time, I did my best to show an interest in Uncle Al's abortive novel and tried to suppress what I really thought of it under a mask of discursive verbiage on what little I knew as to what constitutes good writing. And now that I think of it, I too have often been the object of this same kind of dissembling by visitors whose obvious negative responses to my paintings were transparently concealed behind a barrage of enthusiasm for the technical problems involved in the work.

I don't know what has become of the Levys. The last I knew, they were settled comfortably in the sunshine of Florida. Perhaps Alexander M. has found other means than writing to find his way back to Highbelow. And I fondly hope that he has been able to take his hard-headed, but loyal little Hana with him.

▣ ▣ ▣

As THIS CHRONICLE ENTERS the year of 1928 and I look back upon the puzzled, almost chaotic state of mind with which I faced the future on my return to New York, I am compelled to take stock of what has been written. As far as I am able, I will continue to bring to light certain compelling objectives which have kept me at this manuscript in spite of my misgivings as to whether it will ever become a readable book.

How does one, coming from beginnings such as mine, manage time and experience to generate the will and to find the inner power to grow and change bit by bit, from an acquired form of being into a new and self-generating condition of seeing and understanding that finally repudiates one's own worldly origins? Perhaps I should use the word *repudiate* with a certain caution. For while I have rid myself of most worldly aspirations and ways of life inherent in the genteel philistinism that engulfed my boyhood and early youth, I still cling to certain ingrained habits and mannerisms that mark me as a product of that syndrome of vacuous conventions and contrived identities from which I would like to feel totally liberated. I am, I must admit, as vain about my appearance and as conventional in my sartorial inclinations as I was as a Yale sophomore. I am as proud of as I am comfortable in the smooth elegance and mechanical excellence of our new automotive import from France. These little weaknesses, when now and then I consider them, make me wonder if I have come as far along the road back to Highbelow as I like to think. Still, I console myself with the rather weak rationalization that a conventional facade is only different from a rebellious, anti-conventional facade, in kind and not in fact. In short, one has to remain a small part of this silly world, the better to get away from it.

▣ ▣ ▣

It WAS IN EARLY JANUARY of 1928 that the great liner, *Majestic*, eased into its berth at its dock in lower Manhattan. My friends and family were there to welcome me and to celebrate my homecoming. My arrival in New York co-incided with the peak of the so-called Whoopee Era, reflecting the inane and irresponsible gyrations of a pleasure surfeited and happily lawless society. New York, with its thousands of speak-easies mocking the pieties of Prohibition morality, was patronized by a citizenry that joined hands with boot-leggers and underworld criminals and together made a shambles of the law of the land. It was a moment of high gaiety, social hypocrisy, heavy drink-ing, and shallow joys. Even the day's most articulate critic, Henry L. Mencken, had to make himself into a literary clown to be heard.

This was the moral and intellectual climate that I proceeded to settle into, not at its edges or periphery but smack in the smoldering center of it. It was hardly the time or place to strengthen the purpose of an all too con-fused and susceptible young man in search of his soul. Surrounded by this fascinating hedonistic jungle that welcomed me all too eagerly, I found himself trapped within the neurotic dichotomy of two mutually exclusive ways of life — one empty and self-destructive, the other self-liberating, heal-ing, and redemptive.

My father had taken a rather posh furnished apartment on 58th Street, a few doors from the Plaza Hotel, a stone's throw from the theater district and the midtown concentration of speak-easies and nightclub life. This was, as I knew, my father's way of indulging my sister who, at the age of twenty-three, was a beautiful young woman with a totally self-consuming fascina-tion for everything that the sizzling night life of Manhattan offered.

After clearing customs with the pockets of my overcoat stuffed with small bottles of contraband scotch whiskey, I assembled my friends at our tempo-rary home where my father, with his never failing sense of humor which al-ways surfaced at the first sign of family trouble, described my exodus from the business world as a matter of Bob, "giving up his job because it inter-fered with his work," my work in his mind having something vaguely to do with writing. And it was no more puzzling to him, poor man, than it was to me. I only knew that I carried around within me an undiscovered world of thought and feeling that, in spite of everything, would not be ignored. I did not know where it would lead nor how to begin my search. But begin I did, with the kind of blind faith and self-belief that only a madman or a hope-lessly illusioned and inexperienced youth would be capable of under the circumstances.

My father, with his rare good nature and understanding, stood aside and encouraged me to find my own way, for better or worse. I was not aware that his own affairs had not been going well, and he made no issue of the fact that my dependence upon him for the first time was becoming a worrisome burden. He had always been proud of his own self-made independence, and he wanted to give me the freedom to follow the same path. Having never felt the securities that come with the sheltering presence of a mother, I didn't realize until much later in life how my father's great spirit provided the strength to eventually rebuild the fearfully shattered beginnings of my life.

My first step was to have a talk with my old friend M.D.C. Crawford. He received me in his cluttered office surrounded by the crowded workrooms where his young female assistants were busy on his many design research projects. Morris gave me a hearty welcome and somehow let me know, without actually saying so, that he was not surprised to see me, and was in fact somewhat relieved that I had been able to disentangle myself from the very business world from which he, himself, had never completely escaped, the world that was holding him a privileged and even honored, if rebellious, prisoner. Morris Crawford, at the moment, personified to me an honorable, if incomplete and compromising, solution to my own painful dilemma. I found the Crawford design enclave on the top floor of the rickety old building on East 13th Street a haven of humanistic strength and integrity undefeated by the proximity and pressures of pragmatic society.

And so I asked him if there might still be a place for me in some corner of his office where I might be allowed to make myself useful in one way or another. Morris knew of the success of my London fabric design projects and was actually less interested in the finished result than in the fact that it had been independently initiated, undertaken, and completed. I suppose if he was asked what he valued most in life, his answer would not be found in the outer, easily visible perimeters of a man's character, but rather in the inner fortitude with which he maintained the freedom of his mind and empathy of spirit, no matter what the circumstances of his life might be. When he had spoken admiringly to me of John Masefield, it was not of the poet per se, but of the man with inner resources powerful enough to write poetry while living the life of a bartender in a Bowery saloon.

In answer to a letter I wrote from London expressing my pent-up anger and disgust with Jack Murdock's artificial world, I received the following:

> My dear Robert:
>
> Once every few years I indulge in a little illness. It seems that my vulnerable heel is my throat, and this time it got me. I got to a hospital: they did their stuff and I escaped only to go back worse. Then I

escaped again, only to be caught by Elizabeth and Fifi, who became my jailers at the all too horrible Fifth Avenue Hotel. Now I am home resting, playing with "Rags" and cutting needless parts out of a book I am at work on. Even a Ford needs new parts and unfortunately, there are none for the human variety.

Into this conflicting mess your letter came.

You must learn to separate your real self from the stuffed lay figure that eats and sleeps, sees and feels things and meets people. Murdock is just one of the "things" that are. He shows you a crude picture of what he wants you and the "lousy" world he believes is life to think he is. Under it all there is a desire for surface culture, social position and wealth that does not exist. There is constant friction. He has to eat crow all the time, pretend, evade, swallow sour things, little slights, etc. that would make a dog gag. Naturally he takes it out on anyone he can. You look easy to him. Remember: a slave's slave lives a hell of a life.

But these things have nothing to do with you. Diamonds are found in muck; pearls are the disease of an oyster; fields grow fertile when spread with manure. Man is small potatoes and few in a hill.

If I looked at my own weary life as it really is—measured it by standards that are accepted—I should wither away. All my life these sordid, pitiful things have clogged me down. I have been in revolt as long as I can remember. And worse than all, I have seen my way out many times so clearly as a man in a desert sees a mirage. After all, the real ego in my cosmos has remained untouched.

In some degree I have become the captain of my soul. That is, I direct a little, allowing for wind and tide the part of me that counts to me.

All men feel these things to some degree. This accounts, perhaps, for religion—an attempt to arrange values unaffected by life's standards. There is in all hearts that luring hope, and old forms and creeds exist in spite of intellects because of this dual character in men. It accounts for the interest in art, literature and the drama—even scholarship, since men lose their everyday drabness by delving into things, though outside the deadly empire of the passing hour. The old man of the sea is on every shoulder—a little.

Rare men have been able to make the distinction. Pere Marquette had so schooled himself that he smiled at the gleam of Paradise even while the Iroquois squaws tortured him. His "real" body was conquered

149

and held apart from his inner sense of glory. Well, we are all like that a little—must learn to smile and be indifferent to crude assaults on our true selves.

The soul is the place to which we retire—our citadel of safety from the banal and sordid. Learn to pull the hole in after you. It is not like a gaudy muffler we wear about our neck. No one must know of your retreat.

Think just a little what it cost Mark Twain's fine, lucid mind and sensitive nature to rub elbows with his world. Remember Conrad's years of misery he turned into golden pages; Stevenson's illness; Melville's lack of sympathy. Prendergast lived in a garret aloof from the world and put his soul in paint; Ryder lived a gloomy hermit wrapped in his greater vision. It was never easy. It can never be easy; it must only look easy. No one must see in a work of art the misery and effort of the artist. Become then tolerant outwardly; taste life; take in form and expression; look at the sunlight.

If you can get on familiar footing with your own self, there are not enough fools born to bother you.

Affectionately,

MORRIS

Still, there was the other face of this complex character that could suddenly embrace what would appear on the surface as a kind of crudely aggressive anti-intellectualism as soon as the inner life that he valued was used as a shelter against facing up to and surmounting the demands of social realities. In an earlier letter to me when I was working as a reporter for the Fairchild newspapers, in response to my request for his opinion of a short story I had written, he said in part:

...Right now you look at the job as a matter of phrase making. This will make you very indignant and I hope it does.... If you are going to write sufficiently well to melt the self-consciousness of readers, to magic them out of their own concentrated selfishness sufficiently for them to lay down the burden for that which must live in the illusion you have created, if I may say so, this is a hell of a job!...

Paper is cheap, you can steal pencils, and you don't need a catcher, as a left-handed pitcher does. Hence, go to it and the more you write the less it will please you until you learn to write in such a way that image, expression and continuity of idea at last please you.

...Remember this: it is a good deal more important to be a man than to be an artist and a man is not demonstrated by his weaknesses, and it is quite possible to be happy and successful in the art of living even if you never sign your name to anything but once in a while to a check. I have met more contented, happy salesmen who got a kick out of life and had fun in the Hart, Schaffner & Marx organization than I have met happy, satisfied, contented artists in all my life days. Stick that in your hat and once in a while take a look at it!

. . . John Masefield was once a bartender on Sixth Avenue. This invaluable experience the asinine laws of the country have prevented you, for the time, from acquiring. I don't think bootleggin', even though a thrilling occupation, has quite the philosophical possibilities as tending the bar, but I am free to admit that I may be wrong in this, as in many other things. O'Henry served a sentence in jail. But you have the equivalent of this in a reporter's job.

I don't doubt that M.D.C. secretly identified much of the work he did for the philistines of the clothing industry with the Masefield image. Still, when he saw his philosophy of asceticism being used as a corridor of escape, rather than the source of good works, then he would become almost too blatantly voluble in praise of the untroubled contentment to be found in a life of simple-minded conformity. Dear Morris, I am beginning to believe that he was once a towering Highbelovian ancestor of mine who turned to me in this life to help me find my way back to our long lost origins.

◻◻◻

THE WINTER AND SPRING of 1928, from the start of the New Year through the first weeks of June, come back to me vaguely, yet with clearly recalled impressions and experiences here and there emerging one after another with no apparent continuity or even affinity. The time was one of deep inner conflict and indecision compounded by surrender to superficial and self-indulgent distractions and escapes.

I remember days spent at a table in one of Morris Crawford's workrooms, struggling with a New York version of Mayfair Corners, this time using the configuration of the New York skyscrapers instead of the streets of London's West End for my fabric designs. My plan was to repeat my first success with a variation on the same theme called "Skyline Designs" or something like that. It was to be sponsored by the Crawford office for the benefit of clients such as Hart, Schaffner and Marx. This, of course, was an act of wishful desperation, for the fascination of a first time invention did not persist through this self-imitating effort, and after a few weeks the project succumbed to the inescapable inertia of sheer boredom. Automatically, almost compulsively, I found myself turning more and more from my skyline designs and losing myself in a kind of endless doodle based on variations on the human physiognomy.

One day, one of the young female designers in the office stopped by my table, and looking over my shoulder became engrossed in what I was doing. Sitting down next to me, we began to talk. She sifted through the dozens of faces, young and old, male and female, that were mixed up with the few uninspired fabric designs that lay about. Finally, she said to me very seriously, and I remember it well, "Why don't you stop this nonsense with the business world? You're eventually going to carry on with this other thing. Why don't you stop wasting time and get started?"

Why not, I asked myself.

Soon after this, I remember standing at a store window in the Village on my way back uptown from the Crawford office. What caught my attention was a large brick of modeling plasticene and a selection of modeling tools. I did not close my eyes that night, nor for many nights thereafter. I don't remember anything more related to my job, if it could be called that, on the fifth floor at 13th Street.

What returns in clear recall are long nights working until dawn and into daylight, standing at a tall chest of drawers in my small bedroom on 58th Street. I found myself modeling the head of an old man, thrown back as though in agony, quite realistically and, as I thought, true to life. The thing obsessed me. I worked on it night after night and slept off my exhaustion through the days. It must have been several weeks before I felt that the thing was finished. It was a very bad piece of sculpture, but I was pleased with it if only because at last, I had stopped hopping in and out of this forbidding realm and, this time, on entering it, had stayed long enough to finish what I had started. To do this, I had had to leave behind whatever was left of my shattered opportunities in the workaday world of conventional achievement. I don't remember saying good-bye to Morris Crawford. I only know he did not try to stop me. He must have known from the beginning what lay ahead, and that there would be nowhere to hide—nowhere now except in the shadow cast by the inept intensity of an agonized face modeled in plasticene.

The extent of my involvement, one might almost call it enchantment, with the primitive beginnings of sculptured form can be measured by how vague and confused my recollections are of all other facets of the everyday life that surrounded me. The apartment that I shared with my sister (my father had returned to Chicago) served as a meeting place for the endless comings and goings of her friends, male and female, making the rounds of restaurants, theaters, parties, and nightclubs. There were times when I would join these hilarious, dusk-to-dawn excursions. I even remember two of the wildly popular theatrical hits of the moment. One was the play *Burlesque*, which I believe launched Barbara Stanwick, with her frozen face and magnetically warm body, into an acting career of endlessly successful mediocrity.

The shows I attended were good to distract me long enough to forget myself and my troubling thoughts for the moment. I also remember vividly the basement night club where Jimmie Durante, with his partners Clayton and Jackson, made up a comedy team that produced the kind of hilarious laughter that finally becomes physically painful.

These and other such distractions made up the social and cultural climate that surrounded me. It was from the center of this fascinating syndrome that I was to decide what direction my, as yet, quite aimless life was to take. I cannot say that I did not enjoy the exhilaration of these inane and artificial gaieties. But my enjoyment was tempered by a deep sense of misplacement, by a feeling of entrapment where I did not belong. The person that I was becoming was not me. Lost as I was, I at least recognized that much.

And so I found a room of my own. I don't remember what led me to a tall building on Lexington Avenue in the midtown area known as the Alberton House, but there I moved into a very small room on one of the highest floors with a panoramic view of Manhattan. The place provided the cheapest respectable lodgings to be found outside of the YMCA. And while it accommodated both men and women, the sexes were segregated on separate floors. There was just enough space in the room for a narrow bed, a small desk-like table and chair, and a washstand. It was a grim and dingy set-up compared to the fashionable, well-appointed apartment on 58th street, but it had two advantages that the other lacked—it gave me total privacy and a breathtaking view from my window.

I am trying to remember what I hoped to accomplish in these cramped little quarters in the sky. It is plain that I could not have had any intention of continuing my modeling experiment in these circumstances. And though I had recently done some sporadic writing in the form of fragmentary notations, I had nothing specific in mind to begin work on. It seems to me now that I chose this escape in order to take one deep, cleansing breath, to discover who I was and what was on my mind. I did much thinking and filled pages with notes and scribblings. What little remains from these confused efforts got tucked into the pocket of my suitcase when I packed my few belongings and returned to Chicago to join my father.

◫◫◫

A FEW DAYS AGO, on December 28 1975, I received a cabled message from my old friend, Eddy Ehrich in Tahiti who was observing his seventieth birthday. It read: "By God I made it. What do we do now?"

What *do* we do now? I am unable to paint for reasons that are both obvious and obscure, but in any case are not worth delving into here. My life as I look back, seems dull and certainly not of the stuff that makes for good storytelling. I have had my share of romantic attachments and sexual encounters. I have known the pleasures of strong friendships and the cruelties of human hatred and deceptions. I have been married three times to three worthy ladies but happily, finally, only to the third whom I treasure above all people. I have a daughter whom I love, a step son of whom I am proud, and a son who is not only rarely endowed as an artist, but is one of the earth's good, kind, and hope-inspiring people.

But these are not considerations that brought me to these pages, and they will not influence or intrude into what will follow except in so far as they serve the search for the self-identity that has been the central mystery of my life. In the course of writing these pages, I have often asked myself why I should presume that people would want to read such unfocused and subjective meanderings that bypass most of the usual life experiences that one expects from an autobiographical narrative. I did not set out to fashion a story out of my life here on earth when I decided to add to the Highbelovian manuscript upon discovering it years ago. My purpose was to untangle and set straight the circumstances, experiences, and considerations that induced and shaped the self-metamorphose that has brought me from the chaos of the lost identity of my beginnings to the plateau of old age where I have been able to recapture a glimpse, at least, of the good life I left behind so long ago in Highbelow.

This is perhaps too subjective and self-centered an objective to provide the ingredients for a readable book. But for better or worse, I must try to finish what has been started.

◫◫◫

IT WAS THE LATE SPRING or early summer of 1928 when I joined my father in a pleasant apartment high up in the Sisson Hotel on the south side of Chicago overlooking Lake Michigan. The Sisson was a comfortable, well-appointed residential hotel that provided all the necessary services, including an elegant first floor restaurant with enormous windows that looked out upon a rocky breakwater over which waves smashed when the wind was high, sending up clouds of spray. During the dinner hour, a quartet of piano and strings would play quiet music. The spacious, high-ceilinged room was never crowded, and the few diners would come and go almost unnoticed. There was an atmosphere of amiable, unhurried gentility about the place that was nearer to my memories of London than to what I had recently left behind in New York.

I was glad to be home, and there was much to talk about and decide upon with my father. What was I to do with my life at this point? What direction was I to take? The only solid evidence I had of a viable future was an employee of a clothing manufacturing firm. This one open arena, after a short trial, I had refused to take. In its stead, I began what was to be a lifelong struggle with the English language to articulate the thoughts and perceptions of a mind that could be said to have grown up overnight without the help of skills and disciplines that shape the products of a fully matured intellect. The confusion was compounded by the presence of an irresistible fascination with image making in drawing and modeling. There was, as yet, no convincing evidence of innate gifts as either a writer or artist to justify a try at one profession or the other. But I was so enchanted, if not overwhelmed, with the fragmented manifestations of my first bumbling efforts in both these fields that, in my innocence, I could see no reason why my life's work could not combine the two.

My father listened to me with understanding and responded to my determination to write and draw and sculpt with good-humored approval. His belief in my abilities and me was as automatic as his own unshakable belief in himself. He spoke little of himself, and it must be for this reason that I remember so clearly his telling me repeatedly, with absolute conviction, and a touch of regret, that there was nothing in this world he could not achieve if once he put his mind and hand to whatever was required of him. He believed, very simply and without boasting, that with him all things were possible. And in this sense, I believe he looked upon me as a worthy extension of himself with better opportunities to exercise the gifts with which we were mutually endowed.

If this could be said to be even partially true, it has not been an unmixed blessing in my case, for in accepting the challenges that have come my way, in different and often conflicting fields of endeavor, I have perhaps sacrificed maximum attainment in any one, by overwhelming myself with the effort to master them all. My friend, Maholy [-Nagy] overreached himself in this same way by taking Leonardo as his patron saint. Mark Rothko often chided me for the diversevness of my professional life, calling it a form of schizophrenia that he was thankful to be free of. Sandy Calder was equally disapproving. I have always envied Sandy's monolithic detachment from interests and pursuits that were not central to his "shop." When not working, if he was not eating, drinking, dancing, or conviving, he would sleep easily and instantly wherever he happened to be, even through the sound of voices in serious conversation. Sandy, in his single-minded self-containment, throughout the years of our friendship, has never managed to quite hide a touch of contempt for my multifaceted professional life. After staring silently at some recent paintings in a rare visit to my studio one day, he gruffly asked me why I did not try to find a manner of painting that people would like to buy. I am sure he attributed my failure to find a market for my work to the time wasted in my other activities.

I doubt whether foreknowledge of the difficulties and frustrations that were to plague and exhaust me through the years would have persuaded me to choose one way and stay with it. It really was not a matter of choice. The split was there from the beginning. Perhaps it was preordained. For what it is worth, my rising sign is Gemini. A dear, old astrologer, Ferdie Oslertog, once blamed it all on that. I have always half believed him.

◫ ◫ ◫

ASIDE FROM NOTATIONS on random thoughts and readings scribbled on scraps of paper and in pocket notebooks, I was mainly preoccupied at first with the mysteries of two-dimensional imagery, discovering for myself the true nature of the act of drawing and of the aesthetic ingredient that distinguishes a mere life likeness from an artifact. I was quite unaware of this phenomenon when, in Scotland, I tried to bring to life the cottage I was painting rather than the painting of the cottage. Later, in London (I think) I became vaguely aware of this distinction without really understanding it, through the two copies I made of the drawings by Leonardo and Michelangelo. The sheer power of the drawing itself, in both cases, absorbed the living, breathing reality, transforming it into a new essence. The persistent and deeply felt presence of life only served to confirm the overwhelming dominance of the image of art. Here was the same aesthetic essence that I had found undiluted and self-evident in the art of primitive peoples, but now it was surfacing in Western art, partially obscured to me by the distractingly pervasive mirage of reality.

It was in one of my first drawings, from a window overlooking Lake Michigan, that I met this age-old dichotomy head on and disposed of it then and there, once and for all. I cannot say what was the specific catalyst that cleared my vision and revealed a new and liberating starting point. Looking down one morning at the rocky breakwater that stretched northward along the lake's shore, I saw a dredging barge moored alongside, almost directly under my eyes. It was not that I suddenly saw the visual reality of the boat as something other than what it was, a charcoal drawing, for instance. I did not preconceive a new charcoal image for it. I simply set about, with a strange new sense of confidence and freedom, to use the boat that was moored to the breakwater as the source of clues to the physically and visually felt identity of the marks, one following the other, made by the charcoal, freed of the need to be dissolved into a believable living image of the real thing. With ease, the boat became, before my astonished eyes, a cluster of tones, lines, and marks that confirmed and, strangely, exalted the existence of the boat in a way that the mere everyday sight of it could never do. In one miraculous effort I had discovered the secret of the true relation of the fact and the artifact. With this drawing I became an artist, and I never questioned my right to that identity. That summer I reached the age of 23. It did not occur to me that, in the age-old tradition of the artist's craft, I was getting a very late start.

I was on my way back to Highbelow.

◫ ◫ ◫

[1]See:

Kazin, Alfred. "New York from Melville to Mailer." Partisan Review 47.1 (1981): 85-95.

[2]Holton, Gerald. Thematic Origins of Scientific Thought: Kepler to Einstein. Cambridge, MA: Harvard University Press, 1988.

I've hoarded my work through all these years mostly because I've perhaps over-valued it. Only a few museums own paintings. . . generally, for an old geezer of 72 I'm not well represented around. . . .

I really don't miss the fireworks of fame and exhibitionism—but I do miss the satisfaction of knowing people are sharing my involvement and pleasure with the paintings.

—Robert J. Wolff, November 21, 1977